THRIVING TOGETHER

COUPLE COMMUNICATION II

Sherod Miller, Ph. D.
Phyllis A. Miller, Ph. D.

First Printing: January, 2000

Illustrated by Barrie Maguire
Graphic Assistance: Don Babcock

**INTERPERSONAL
COMMUNICATION
PROGRAMS, INC.**

**30752 Southview Drive
Evergreen, CO 80439
Phone: 1-800-328-5099**

Introduction

Most couples dream of thriving together. In the complex world in which we live, it takes more than a dream to achieve this. As you and your partner attend to and nurture your relationship, you increase your ability to thrive. The COUPLE COMMUNICATION II program and this workbook are designed to support your efforts. The program helps you and your partner:

- Reinforce your talking and listening skills.
- Better understand and strengthen your relationship
- Incorporate collaborative communication into everyday exchanges
- Manage your own anger better
- Respond to your partner's anger effectively
- Reduce conflict
- Align your values and wants
- Enjoy each other more

WHO THIS BOOK IS FOR

This book is geared for couples who have read *Talking and Listening Together* and participated in COUPLE COMMUNICATION I. The advanced program, *Thriving Together:* COUPLE COMMUNICATION II, builds on the foundation laid in the earlier course, and assumes an understanding of and some facility with the frameworks, skills, and processes in *Talking and Listening Together.* It is for partners who want to continue to learn jointly and thrive together in their journey through life.

COUPLE COMMUNICATION II MATERIALS

Each couple uses a COUPLE COMMUNICATION II Packet. (If you take a class, your instructor will tell you how to obtain the CC II Packet.) This packet includes:

- Two copies of this workbook, Thriving Together
- Two laptop skills mats
- Two Awareness Wheel note pads

These materials help you continue to practice and apply the skills plus you learn new ways to combine them to help your relationship thrive.In this advanced course, you will also practice with the large floor skills mats from COUPLE COMMUNICATION I, so be sure to bring these to class with you. In addition, keep your *Talking and Listening Together* workbooks handy for review, as this program builds on and refers to ideas presented there.

Acknowledgements

Thriving Together has grown from the feedback of thousands of participants in COUPLE COMMUNICATION I and the instructors who have taught them. Its ideas are also supported in the richly developing knowledge base about the ingredients of satisfying relationships.

We are grateful to the certified instructors who have piloted this advanced program, giving valuable suggestions and encouragement.

We also want to thank Dr. Daniel Wackman and Dr. Elam Nunnally for their substantial contributions to COUPLE COMMUNICATION and for their friendship over the years.

About the Authors

Drs. Phyllis and Sherod Miller combine their backgrounds in education and training plus marriage and family enrichment and therapy to develop interpersonal communication and conflict resolution programs for couples, work groups, and individuals. While much of their focus is on training and certifying instructors to teach these programs, they also provide direct service to people in business and non-profit organizations. Married for over 37 years, they have two grown children and live in Colorado.

Contents

THE
RELATIONSHIP MAP

Understanding and Taking Charge of
Our Relationship Dance

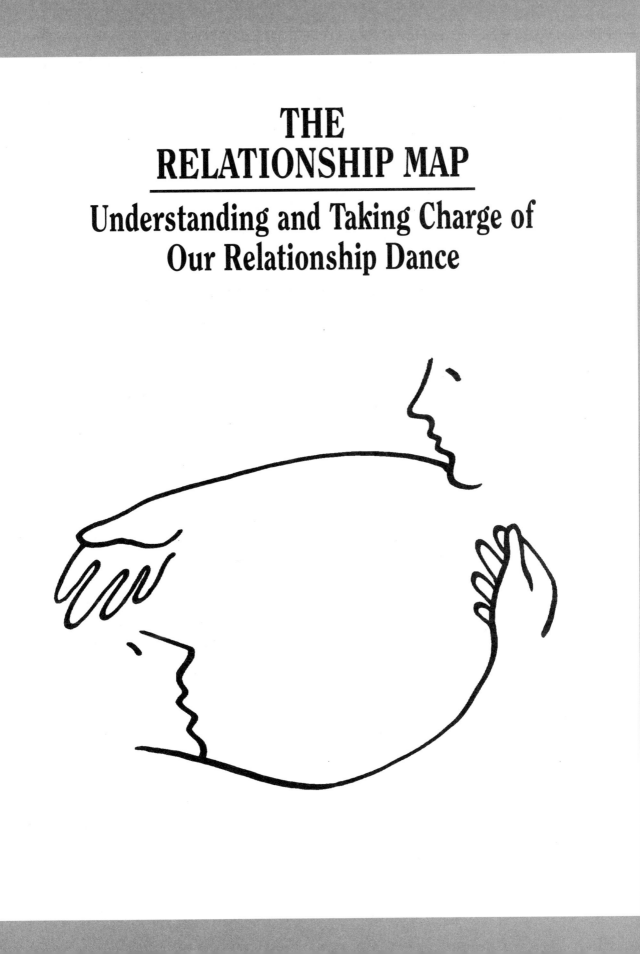

1

Our Relationship Map

As you and your partner discover a map of your relationship, you will understand your partnership better. This will help you set direction for how you relate, so that you can enjoy greater satisfaction, viability, and intimacy in your life as a couple.

The Relationship Map provides perspective of your experience with your partner in specific situations over time. The map encompasses three relational positions: being together, changing, and being apart; it shows that within any of these positions, a climate develops, which may be mainly positive or mainly negative.

Think of the position of being together as being in sensory contact in some way with your partner. For instance, you may be literally face to face, do an activity across the room from one another, or be far from each other yet talking by phone. The position of changing captures what goes on in your relationship as you and your partner initiate and respond to transitions.

The position of being apart refers to times when you are out of sensory contact. For example, you can think of you and your partner as being apart although you are in the next room from one another, or you can consider being apart as a separation of great actual physical distance.

The climate at any point in time primarily concerns how you feel about how you relate, however, climate is influenced by all parts of your Awareness Wheel. In a positive climate, you mainly feel *confident* and *comfortable* with yourself and your partner. In a negative climate, you mainly feel *uncertain* and *anxious* about yourself and your partner.

As a conceptual guide, The Relationship Map helps you and your partner:

- Become more aware of the positive and negative ways you relate and the impacts upon your relationship.

- Take better charge of your life as a couple — see choice points for making your exchanges more positive.

- Savor and appreciate your relationship.

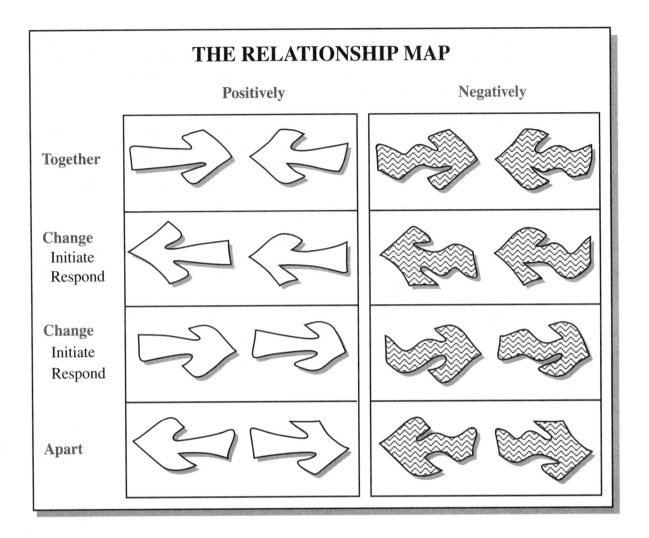

THE RELATIONSHIP MAP

(Positively — Negatively columns; rows: Together, Change Initiate Respond, Change Initiate Respond, Apart)

TOGETHER AND APART

It is useful to take a closer look at each part of The Relationship Map. To do that, begin with the positions of being together and of being apart, both in positive climates. Next, move to those positions in negative climates. Following that, view what occurs both positively and negatively during change. The whole map incorporates what you learned in COUPLE COMMUNICATION I.

TOGETHER POSITIVELY

In this position, with a positive climate, you probably experience a number of the following dimensions.

Caring Attitude

Both you and your partner, in either small or large ways, display an underlying attitude of taking one another into account, of respecting self and the other, and of valuing yourselves. Your behavior expresses the assumption that each of you has significance.

Variety of Styles of Communication But No Use of Style II

How you talk and how you listen may have considerable variety when you are together in a positive climate. You use Small Talk or Shop Talk and Conventional Listening, as you connect. In Style I you relax, have a pleasant conversation, or update each other and exchange new information. Some couples enjoy a time of Search Talk and Explorative Listening as they ponder possibilities or discuss an issue. You move into Straight Talk when you share intimacies. You also apply Straight Talk, as well as Attentive Listening, when something serious is at hand, and the use of this style helps to keep the climate positive. Style II is not part of your experience when you are together in this way.

Satisfactory Resolutions to Conflict

In any relationship issues occur, which sometimes lead to conflicts. If you and your partner experience being together positively when there is conflict, you probably do so because you are able to work through the conflict to a satisfactory outcome. You may also sense that the process itself, though perhaps difficult, is productive in the way you have brought about the resolution, and it leaves you feeling good about one another.

Impact of Being Together Positively

If you are like most couples, you are drawn to the positive aspects of being together — freely sharing thoughts, feelings, wants, playing, joking, touching, praying, celebrating, deciding, creating something, or just relaxing in comfortable silence — enjoying each other's company. Even if your time together involves working through difficult issues, you care enough to find mutually satisfying solutions. As these events accumulate, you experience cohesion and bonding. A unique *we-ness* and *us-ness* develops.

Freedom and belonging develop in these shared moments and experiences. Emotional openness and physical closeness create a safe haven and a secure base. Here you can share your authentic self — one that is not always known to others outside your partnership. You become intimate, which is sometimes defined as knowing each other's vulnerabilities and choosing not to hurt one another.

As you develop intimacy, you attend to and affirm one another, which build self and other esteem. These attitudes and behaviors are invigorating and provide a source of contentment in life. Generally, evidence shows that they also positively influence your health and lengthen your life.[1]

APART POSITIVELY

When you and your partner are apart from one another, and you experience a positive climate within your relationship, it is so because several elements are in effect. These keep you feeling comfortable and secure with your relationship.

Caring Attitude

Even though you are not together, you and your partner demonstrate a caring attitude toward one another and the relationship in the ways you behave. You recognize and honor the boundaries of your relationship and maintain the trust each places in the other. Your words and actions show congruency with your commitments to your absent partner.

Beliefs and Wants Coincide (About Relationship)

Though apart, you and your partner each hold the expectation that you will re-connect, and you both have the desire to be together again. Neither believes that the time away, for whatever reason, threatens the relationship.

Individual Pursuits Accepted

You each willingly accept the other as pursuing some individual experiences, for career, leisure activity, or personal growth. You recognize that you each have certain separate interests and strengths, and that participating in activities beyond your relationship brings enjoyment to whichever one is involved. You both agree that these pursuits develop you personally as individuals, without diminishing or detracting from your partnership, and both are supportive of the activities.

Time Out

As you recall from COUPLE COMMUNICATION I, Time Out refers to the option of one or both partners calling for a break from an extended, unproductive, or overwhelming (mentally or emotionally) conversation. This is done in order to re-balance, gain privacy, or reflect individually on an issue at hand. Both of you respect and comply with this call, recognizing that it is temporary, and confident that the issue will be revisited in a mutually accountable way.

Impact of Being Apart Positively

Regardless of the reason you and your partner are apart from one another, whether for purposes of work or for individual interests, being away from one another serves as a resource for your relationship as a whole. Your apartness contributes something helpful for you both — ideas, experiences, or finances.

Also, after you have been apart, your time together becomes more interesting and stimulating. Your conversations may be more energized, as each shares what has gone on in your separate circumstances. Perhaps you just draw closer together as you talk about your individual situations. Being apart positively makes you able to enrich one another generally.

If you have been apart because either of you has called Time Out, your reconnecting is probably more productive. You each may have gained some perspective or awareness that helps you take whatever brought on the call to a new level. This may be another step in understanding and resolving an issue, simply an agreement to disagree about something, or a decision to live with an issue unresolved.

TOGETHER NEGATIVELY

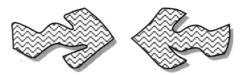

In this relationship position, with a negative climate, you probably experience some of the following elements. These give rise to your feelings of uncertainty and anxiety about your relationship.

Uncaring Attitude

One or both of you holds a discounting attitude toward the other and possibly toward self. Lack of respect for and de-valuing of one another and the relationship comes out in the behavior, which expresses the assumption that, either momentarily or longer term, the other is not important.

Predominant Use of Negative Style II Communication

In this position, your talk falls mainly into Fight Talk and Spite Talk styles. You focus on "speaking for other," include many "you shoulds" and "you oughts," and ask "why" questions. Your words and tones of voice signal frustration, tension, or anger. Whether your language is directly aggressive and defensive or indirectly aggressive and defensive, your messages attempt to control the other.

Listening is reactive. It shuts out genuine awareness of the other partner, by either of you formulating internally your own reaction while your partner talks, or by interrupting to counter or twist what is said. In this state, arguments and fights ensue.

It is also possible in this negative position that you do not talk much at all when you are together, except for certain necessary Shop Talk comments. Small Talk disappears, contributing to the general sense of disaffection and tension. Nonverbal behaviors, such as banging doors, convey anger or disgust, as well.

Unsatisfactory or No Resolutions to Conflicts

When issues arise that bring conflict between the two of you, you are unable to reach a resolution that would be satisfying to both. You may avoid dealing with the issue. Or an argument arises, and if one of you finally capitulates, you do so resentfully or attempt to continue the conflict under the surface. Your conflicts may reach impasses from which you are unable to pull out, or your outcomes leave one or both feeling upset.

Impact of Being Together Negatively

As you spend time together negatively, tearing each other down, it tends to lower the self esteem of one or both of you. This diminishing may carry over into other areas of life as well, contributing to an overall discontentment, lack of productivity, and general hesitancy about personal value.

On-going, pervasive negative emotions that result from your experiences with one another can translate into health problems. You can suffer physically, as well as mentally or emotionally, and this can shorten your life expectancy.[2]

Finally, too much negative togetherness prevents intimacy and ultimately threatens the relationship itself.

APART NEGATIVELY

When you and your partner are apart from one another, and you experience a negative climate for your relationship, it is probably so because several elements are in effect. These keep you feeling anxious and uncertain about your relationship.

Uncaring Attitude

When you are not together, one or both of you demonstrates an uncaring attitude toward one another and disregards the relationship in the ways you behave. You or your partner may overstep the boundaries of your relationship, and whether secretly or not, do things that undermine the trust being placed in you by the other partner. Words and actions discount or are incongruent with commitments made to your relationship.

Beliefs and Wants Diverge (About Relationship)

When apart, you and your partner may hold different expectations about your ability to re-connect in intimate ways. One may believe that being connected is not important to the relationship, while the other does. One or the other partner may not desire to be together again or may dread it. One thinks that the time away is a threat to the relationship, while the other may consider it as a relief from the relationship.

Individual Pursuits Resented

One or both of you tries to prevent, or merely tolerates, it when the other participates in an individual activity. The separate pursuit is upsetting to or resented by the remaining partner, and the one who does it feels guilty or irritated about what it takes to do it. A stubborn stand or manipulation may occur by either of you to get your own way.

Withdrawal

This occurs when one of you backs away from contact with the other, and the remaining partner is not agreeable with the backing away at the time. When the withdrawal happens, one or both of you probably lacks confidence that any issue that might be at hand can be faced again or revisited in a mutually accountable way.

Impact of Being Apart Negatively

Regardless of the reason you are apart from one another, when you are in this emotional climate, being apart drains the relationship reservoir. The emptying reveals scars and leaves debris.

The high levels of anxiety regarding your relationship can interfere with ordinary daily concentration, productivity, and functioning for one or both of you. Other normal activities and relationships are affected. Unless you and your partner are able to compartmentalize, your negative emotional state spreads, possibly infecting people around and diminishing your ability to carry on other parts of life.

Also, when you are separated, various negative feelings, such as jealousy, fear, anger, or hurt can increase from the uncertainty surrounding your situation. These emotions may gain even more strength than when you are together, because you may imagine the worst. Excessive amounts of negativity can lower your general resistance, and you can be more susceptible to fatigue, illness, or accident.[3]

Chronic, negative apartness threatens the relationship and becomes a step toward dissolution. Even when you are together again, it may take enormous amounts of energy to re-connect or repair the damage, and you and your partner may lose the will or strength to do so. It becomes easier to give up on one another, without even engaging negatively. Whether you part in an official, legal way or settle for a distant, disconnected sort of life style, loneliness and a sense of hopelessness often persist.

Evidence indicates that aspects involved with being apart negatively affect your health. Social isolation, alienation and loneliness constitute risk factors for psychological and physical disorders, including cardiovascular disease.[4]

TOGETHER OR APART POSITIVELY

Instructions: Fill out the Awareness Wheel below, to recall an experience of you and your partner being together or being apart positively.

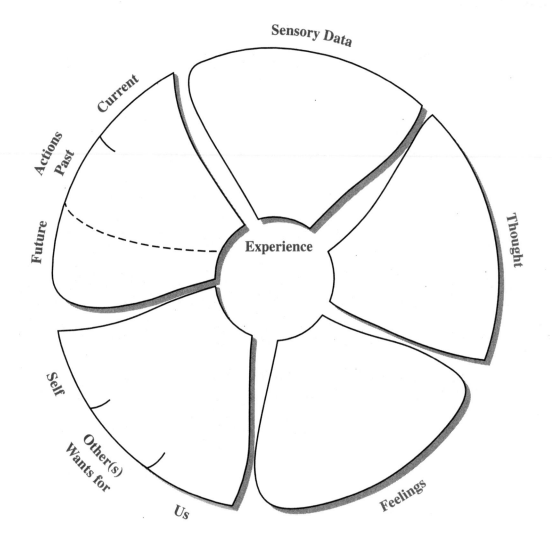

TELL YOUR PARTNER ABOUT YOUR AWARENESS

Instructions: Place your large skills mat on the floor, to share with your partner your awareness of the experience of being together or being apart positively, using the talking skills listed below.

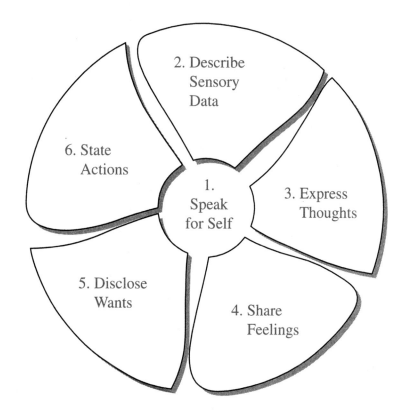

CHANGE — INITIATING AND RESPONDING

Change takes you out of your routine and brings the prospect of shifting your comfort zone, either expanding or threatening it. It holds the potential for creating excitement and interest or for stirring distress and anxiety. How change is experienced — positively or negatively — has to do, in large part, with the processes involved of initiating and responding to it. These initiating and responding processes also have implications for your relationship.

Begin by looking at positive ways either you or your partner may initiate change and positive ways of responding. Then move to negative ways of initiating and responding. The greater the change for the relationship, the more important the manner of initiating and the more intense the response may be. Again, the Map incorporates what you learned in COUPLE COMMUNICATION I.

INITIATING CHANGE POSITIVELY

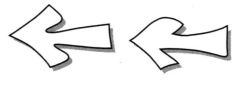

A number of ways exist to initiate change positively, and you may have experienced any of them as the partner who has brought it up or as the one who has responded. Probably some of the following elements have been present to make the climate of the initiation of that change positive.

Appropriate Context

The general context of proposing change influences the level of positive emotion around it. Making sure that the time and place are appropriate to discuss a change is one aspect of initiating it in a positive manner. Privacy may be very important for such a discussion; on the other hand, a public announcement may fit for certain circumstances if it does not embarrass or manipulate the partner. Bringing up a possible change when both of you are fresh (or at least not too tired) also makes a difference. When you have experienced positive initiation of change, think about the context in which it has been done.

Wants for Other and the Relationship

Initiation of a change can be a more positive experience if the partner bringing up the change takes the wants for the other (based on the other's stated interests) into account, besides his or her own wants. Being able to talk accurately about and incorporate the other's interests is essential to positive change. This includes an appraisal of how the change will impact those wants. Talking about wants for the relationship in regard to the proposed change helps make the atmosphere more congenial. Tuning into the wants for the other and for the relationship offers a motivating force for the change.

Speaking for Self

This talking skill makes a message easier to hear, which is particularly important when it is about change. Speaking for self helps you or your partner express your experience (from any zone of the Awareness Wheel) related to the proposed idea in a more gentle way.

Maximizing Choice

The more choice the one who initiates the change offers, the higher the participation will be by the one who responds. This extends to being open to suggestions and exploration of options. When the initiator gains input and tries to discover the best fit for each person, the chances are better for ownership by both of you.

Understanding Partner's Response

Generally, once one partner proposes some sort of change, the other partner responds. Being able to understand that response, which may mean using Attentive Listening skills, shows care for the partner in the situation. This in itself provides a more positive climate when change is initiated.

Impact of Initiating Change Positively

Initiating change allows new information to enter the system and provides opportunity for adaptation, learning, and growth. It gives stimulation for conversation, either just momentarily or the possibility of setting new goals and reevaluating where you are for a longer term. These activities tend to create energy for the relationship.

Any change is potentially destabilizing, but when a change is initiated in a way that produces a positive climate, it is easier on both of you. This feeds the relationship system, which nourishes its robustness and helps it thrive. Contributing to a positive climate helps the well-being of both partners.

Also, the chances for a positive, or at least acceptable, response to the initiator increases. While it does not guarantee such a response, it lowers the risk of a negative exchange.

RESPONDING TO CHANGE POSITIVELY

Once you or your partner has proposed a change in situation, if you experience a positive climate, it may be because any of the following elements have been present in the response.

Supporting the Change

Supporting the change by telling the initiating partner that you agree and are behind whatever is suggested definitely provides a positive response. Actually encouraging it amplifies the feelings that make a positive emotional climate. Also, as responder, even if you are not one hundred percent behind the proposed change, letting the initiator know that you will go along with the change willingly keeps things comfortable.

Understanding the Initiating Partner

If you or your partner has suggested something that would lead in a new direction, demonstrating that the originator's initiative is understood can be significant in making the experience positive. This may mean the responder uses Attentive Listening skills to hear the whole story while his or her concerns are on hold temporarily. Particularly this would include acknowledging and accurately summarizing the proposal. Or it may involve considering the idea without pre-closing by inviting more information. Understanding is the first step in any successful negotiation.

Speaking for Self in Response

Once you or your partner has fully understood the other initiating the change, speaking for self in response contributes to a positive climate. This would be so whether the response is to agree with the change, go along with it, or hesitate about it and offer resistance to it.

Impact of Responding Positively

Responding positively to the desired change initiated by your partner keeps you both moving in the same direction. This helps blend your relationship together and develops a stronger bond between the two of you.

It is wonderful for the initiator to have an idea or to take a step in a new direction and to be supported with no hesitation. Likewise, for the responder, it is interesting or maybe relieving to follow along. When you respond positively to a suggestion from your partner — show interest, grant approval, give support, or even encourage a new initiative — a good experience often results for both of you. If the idea does not turn out as expected, you can comfort or commiserate with one another in your disappointment.

Responding positively to your partner's initiation allows new information to enter your system more easily, and undergirds the potential for added experience, learning, and growth for both. While it seems paradoxical, sometimes going along with change positively helps maintain stability in your partnership.

INITIATING CHANGE NEGATIVELY

Initiating change does not always go so smoothly. Typically some of the following elements exist to make the climate negative — anxious and uncertain for you — as change is proposed.

Inappropriate Context for Initiating the Change

You may have experienced a situation in which you or your partner proposed something new, and the context was all wrong. It was a bad time or place. Maybe one of you was interrupted from some activity that took concentration, and it was brought up in a rushed, urgent way. Perhaps the level of stress or fatigue was high for either of you. Other people were present, when it could have been done in private. Any of these elements contributed to the anxiety generated from it.

Wants For Self Only

When you or your partner initiate change and do so in a way that only addresses wants for self, you increase the likelihood of a negative climate. This occurs whether the wants are spoken or hidden. If the wants for self only are talked about, they come across as selfish or narcissistic, with no concern for wants for the other or the relationship. If the real wants for self are kept quiet, they become hidden agenda, and the apparent actions seem confusing or manipulating to the responding partner.

Speaking for Other

When you or your partner attempts to initiate change by speaking for the other, your message is harder to hear. Speaking for other tends to create its own resistance, which interferes with understanding. For example, in Control Talk, you attempt to take charge to tell your partner what to think or do. When your partner complies, Control Talk works. It is efficient. However, as happens with many couples, your partner may not comply with your Control Talk. Then your exchanges can easily escalate to Fight Talk. Your partner thinks he or she is being boxed in, which increases defensiveness, regardless of what the change may entail.

Minimizing Choice

Any time you limit your partner's participation or actual choices, when initiating change, you are prone to stir negativity. If your responding partner has little or no say in the proposed change or the way it may be brought about, you will dampen the receptivity to it. Being closed to input by your partner about a change that will affect your relationship shows a presumptuous, discounting attitude.

Unskilled Communication Combined with Uncaring Attitude

In this situation, one of you wants to initiate change, and whoever it is does so in a demanding, threatening manner. The goal is to force the change. It may include blaming the other as the reason for the change. Or as initiator, you may feel desperate about your desires. No attempt is made to understand your partner's experience relating to the change.

Impact of Initiating Change Negatively

The initiation of any change has potential for disrupting or destabilizing your partnership, however, when a change is brought up in a way that produces a negative climate, it is even harder on both of you. The chances are greater that the reaction will be one of resistance, perhaps turning into an impasse. This takes energy that could be used more productively to bring about the change. These results may occur, regardless of any ultimate value to the overall relationship system of the proposed idea.

Because of the manner in which the change is brought up, the focus may shift to defending or attacking rather than understanding one another or really evaluating the merits of the new possibility. Animosity can arise, and it may take greater effort to carry through the proposal, if it can be done. Both partners may wind up suffering in some way.

The initiation of change negatively may create a challenge for looking at what is really important to one another in the relationship. It can offer the opportunity to be clear about the interests of each, even if what is discovered is not pleasing to either one. It can highlight choices that have to be made.

RESPONDING TO CHANGE NEGATIVELY

Once you or your partner has proposed a change in situation, regardless of how it was initiated, the response can turn the climate negative. Perhaps you have experienced this, and it is likely the following elements have been present in the response.

Resisting the Change

Resisting the change can take several forms that will turn or keep a climate negative. You or your partner, whoever is the responder, squashes the idea or dream, undercuts it, or immediately counter-proposes something else. You block the idea by criticizing or challenging it with "why" questions, or say it will not work or it is not the thing to do. You indicate you will not comply or go along with the change.

Not Showing Understanding

When a change has been initiated by one of you, and whichever one is responding does not acknowledge the idea or explore it more fully, that demonstrates apparent lack of understanding of the proposed suggestion. This is particularly so in Reactive Listening if the responder interrupts, without really hearing the whole story. Not showing understanding increases the tension, and helps create a negative climate.

Obstructing Passively

This response to an initiation of change includes a form of stonewalling, in which you or your partner demonstrates you will "not respond," either by being silent or by saying something such as, "I don't know what you are talking about." You refuse to share your awareness (or tune into your partner's) about the proposed change. Another type of passive obstructing occurs when the partner responding gives in to the change, but displays a resentful undercurrent and behaves in ways that actually undermine it. For example, the responder places obstacles in the way, makes spiteful comments, or drags the feet to comply.

Impact of Responding Negatively to Change

As frustrating as it may be to the initiating partner, a negative response can operate as an early warning signal to protect against a hasty, poor decision or the wasting of valuable energy and resources. In such a situation, the negative response to a proposed change can serve to maintain boundaries and sustain stability for the relationship. Though unpleasant, it may protect the partnership's overall interests.

However, a negative response may also limit potentially helpful information and thwart useful modification. It can bring about an atmosphere that prevents a clear look at new opportunities.

Perhaps more importantly, a negative response can stifle the pleasure in sharing an idea by the initiating partner, and the disappointment by that partner in not being heard can reduce intimacy between the two. Such a response dampens the possibility for deeper understanding and appreciation of one another. It increases the chance of developing an adversarial rather than a collaborative approach to meeting the challenges of life together.

LISTEN TO AN EXPERIENCE OF CHANGE

Instructions: Place the large listening skills mat on the floor, to listen to your partner's experience of change being initiated positively or negatively by you or your partner, and then being responded to positively or negatively by the other. As you use the listening skills, as shown below, the goal at this point is simply to understand your partner's experience, and not to alter it.

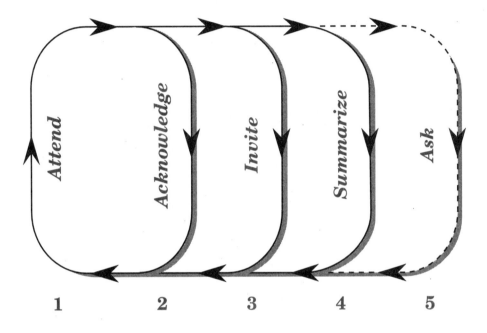

MIXING AND MATCHING

It is possible for you or your partner to initiate a change positively, yet the other person responds negatively. Likewise, you can negatively initiate something new and receive a positive response. Each of you as partners has choice in an exchange about the attitude and the behavior displayed, regardless of whether you are initiating or responding to some type of change for your relationship.

In summary, The Relationship Map allows you to look at the whole of your relationship — being together and apart, as well as initiating and responding to change. Your experiences of these various relational positions generate a particular emotional climate.

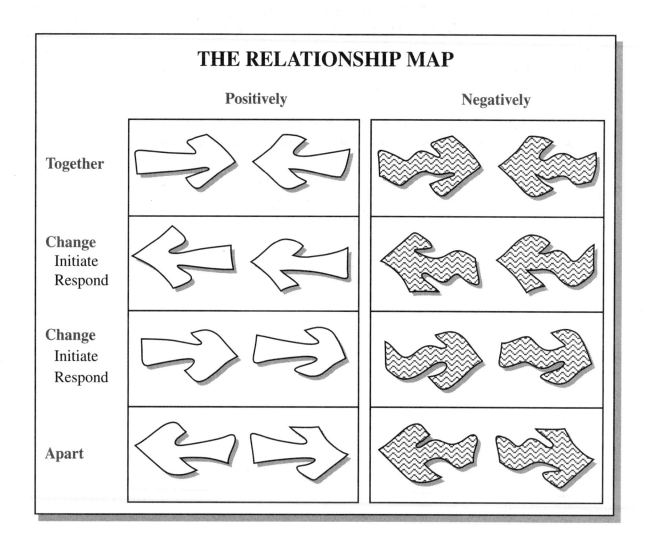

A positive climate occurs when you feel *confident* and *comfortable* about your relationship, and a negative one occurs when you feel *uncertain* and *anxious*.

RELATIONSHIP DANCE

You can think of you and your partner as moving through space and time, around The Relationship Map, in an interpersonal dance. Initially, each of you has brought your own preferred dance steps — ways of relating — to your experience together. You have learned these conscious or unconscious steps early in life from interacting with the important people around you. These moves typically become the basis, or the patterns, for your own dance steps in your partnership. As you have blended, or failed to blend your steps, in pressured and non-pressured situations, you develop your own unique couple dance.

Also, as a couple, you may be changing the way you dance as a result of learning and using new communication skills in COUPLE COMMUNICATION I.

Now as you continue to practice your skills and expand your ways of applying them in COUPLE COMMUNICATION II, you may find it useful to see where you are at this point, in terms of The Relationship Map.

OUR CURRENT RELATIONSHIP DANCE

Instructions: The solid line across both pages represents your relationship boundaries, including both positive and negative interactions.

1. With your partner, choose the same time period to explore. Also decide whose name is to be represented by which arrows.

2. As individuals, assign a per cent to each of the eight states (position and climate) as you have experienced your dance during the time period. The total of the eight

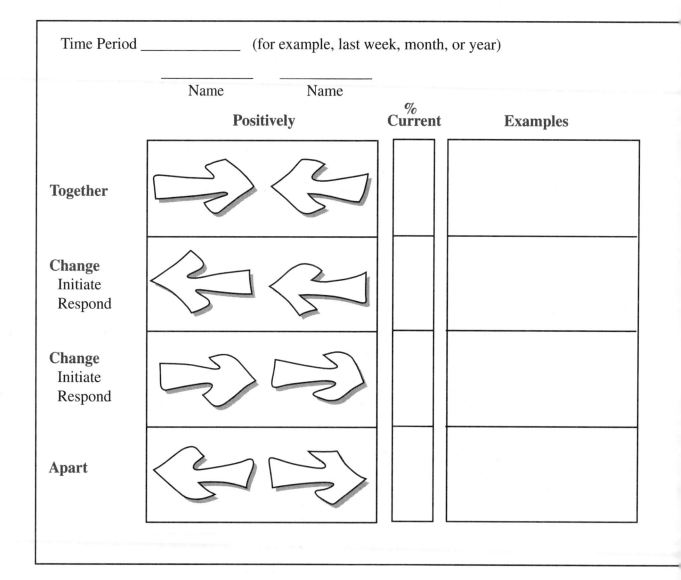

Time Period _____ (for example, last week, month, or year)

	Name	Name	% Current	Examples
	Positively			
Together				
Change Initiate Respond				
Change Initiate Respond				
Apart				

percentages on both pages should sum to 100 percent.

3. Give examples to illustrate your experience of each state.

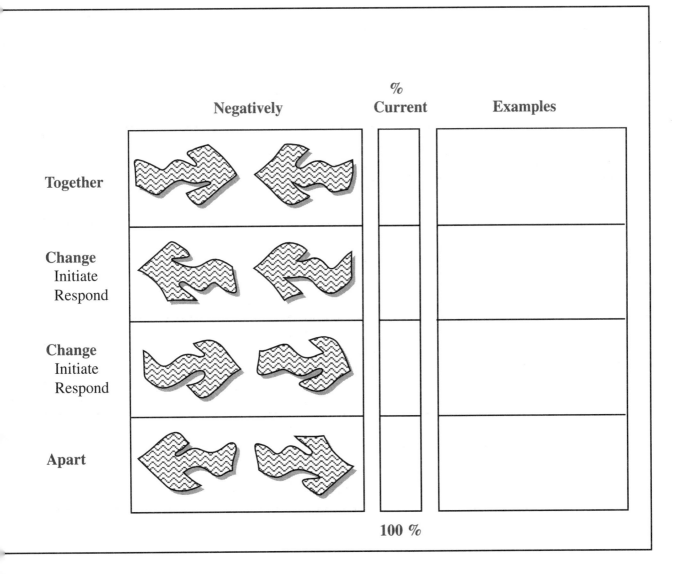

APPLY ALL YOUR SKILLS

In COUPLE COMMUNICATION I, you learned ways to use the large Awareness Wheel and Listening Cycle skills mats. Now, in COUPLE COMMUNICATION II, the addition of small laptop mats will help you use all your skills more readily and conveniently.

The small laptop mat contains both the Awareness Wheel and the Listening Cycle, as shown in the following diagram. As the diagram and your small mat shows, all eleven skills — six talking and five listening ones — are before you. You see the complete set of skills easily at hand.

Use the laptop mat as a reminder of skills to use, or as a way to track your participation in a skilled conversation. This mat is particularly helpful when you deal with an issue.

If you wish, point with your fingers to the skill in use. Choose from any of the skills, in any order, when you and your partner hold a serious discussion, whether you sit across from one another or side by side.

DISCUSS YOUR DANCE

Instructions: Discuss with your partner your current relationship dance in a skilled way, keeping in mind both the talking and listening skills as you converse. Use the small skills mat to prompt you.

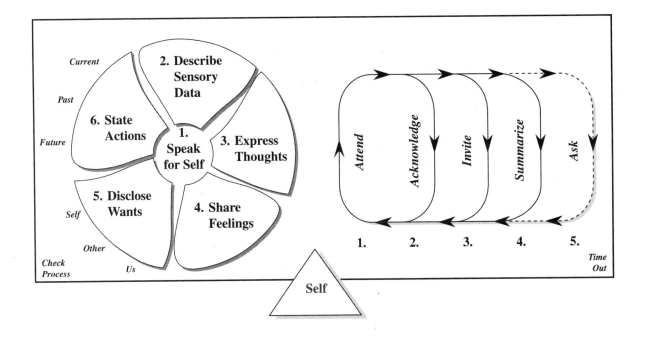

OUR DESIRED RELATIONSHIP DANCE

Instructions:

1. With your partner, choose a time period in the future. Use the same arrows as before (in your current dance) to indicate whose name is to be represented by which arrows.

2. Individually, assign a percent to each state (position and climate), which you desire your relationship dance to be over the time period. The total of all positive and negative states should equal 100 percent.

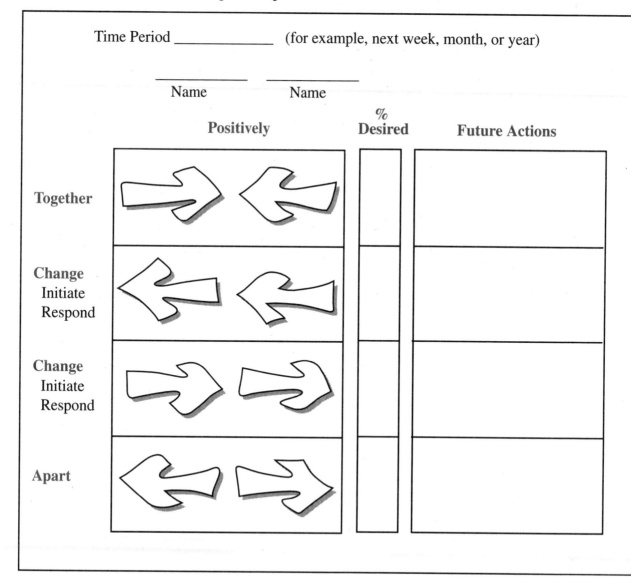

Time Period _____ (for example, next week, month, or year)

_____ _____
Name   Name

Positively   % Desired   Future Actions

Together

Change
Initiate
Respond

Change
Initiate
Respond

Apart

3. Give actions that could help you achieve your desired dance.

4. Compare and discuss your desired dance with your partner, again using the laptop mat to prompt skills.

5. Choose one or two specific actions to take.

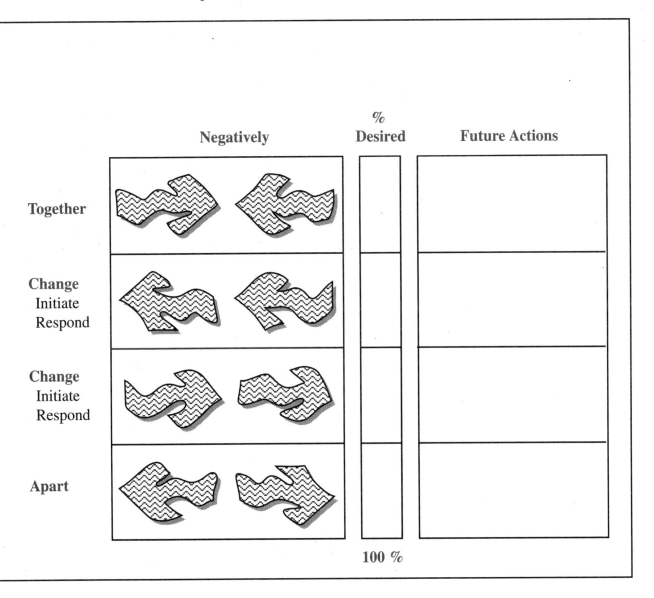

IMPLICATIONS OF THE RELATIONSHIP MAP

Research shows that for couples to thrive together, certain characteristics must be present.[5] These include:

- Positive climate interactions outweigh by far the negative ones.

- Both partners are capable of doing all the steps associated with a positive climate, in any position — together, apart, or initiating and responding to change.

- Both partners are able to take individual responsibility for limiting and shifting out of a negative dance when it occurs.

The 11 communication skills contained in the Awareness Wheel and the Listening Cycle provide a means to alter interactions so they are more positive.

USING YOUR RELATIONSHIP MAP

When you understand your Relationship Map, you can see where to increase your positive experiences with your partner and where to decrease the negative ones. And, you can take actions that help you improve the way you relate.[6] To do so:

- Focus on your own contributions to the emotional climate in the various positions (together, apart, or in change).

- Apply skills to your interactions.

These actions will help you to alter your dance positively.

PARTNER DISCUSSIONS

Preferences

Many partners hold different preferences for positive togetherness and apartness. Discuss, with your partner, your individual preferences for closeness and distance.

Parents' Map

Your parents' Relationship Map — climate and patterns of closeness, distance, and change — has a strong influence, one way or another, on how you relate to your partner.[7] Individuals tend to prefer, and even expect as "normal," what they have experienced while growing up. For some partners, the differing expectations can be a source of conflict if these powerful dynamics are not recognized or understood. Use The Relationship Map on page 24 to:

1. Describe to your partner your view of your parents' Relationship Map.

2. Compare your parents' patterns to your own similar or different preferences and expectations.

OTHER ACTIVITIES

- Use the Relationship Map to help you understand other important relationships in your life, for example, those you have with your child, parent, friend, employee, colleague, or boss.

- Look for a small kindness you can do for your partner each day, and do it.

- Thank your partner for the things that he or she does which make your life easier or more enjoyable.

- Give and receive nurturing, stress-relieving hugs daily. Enjoy the togetherness.

- Tell your partner about the little things he or she does that you enjoy, find fun, or think attractive.

- Share, with your partner on a regular basis, one thing that has gone well for you during the day.

COLLABORATIVE COMMUNICATION

Creating a Process
for Ensuring Satisfying Outcomes

2

Collaborative Communication

In the course of your relationship, you and your partner interact in countless situations, ranging from connecting with one another in Small Talk to exchanging intimacies in Straight Talk. Somewhere in the breadth of interactions are the conversations of importance that arise regularly yet not always predictably.

Situations unfold, and issues arise. Something comes along, and you find yourselves as a couple needing to:

- Make a decision

- Solve a problem

- Plan an activity

- Set priorities

- Schedule an event

As you live your life together, these activities come into play. Depending on what is at stake, the level of importance can range from minor to major, yet the common element is that to some degree you both are involved. Actually, over time, carrying out these types of discussions successfully becomes a significant part of maintaining and building your relationship. Any of them can lead to conflict, yet they also hold the potential for collaboration and deeper understanding and appreciation of one another. The challenge is to keep the climate positive during these occurrences, or if a negative climate enters, to turn it into a positive one.

THE THIRD FORCE

It is helpful to recognize forces at work when you are in one of these discussions — making a decision, solving a problem, planning something, setting priorities, or scheduling an event.

THE FIRST FORCE — CONTENT

When a situation arises for you and your partner that requires one of these types of discussion, the situation contains some form of content. This content includes the related information from the zones of your separate Awareness Wheels, whether either of you is tuned into part or all of this information at the time or not. The content contains the story of your individual experiences concerning the situation.

Content
Information
Experience
(5 Zones)

Situation

THE SECOND FORCE — OUTCOME

As you figure out the situation, you strive to reach a decision, to develop an agreeable, workable solution, or to establish a plan. This is the result to be achieved or the action to take. The outcome is what you aim for as you deal with a situation, and how you evaluate that outcome, to a large degree, is what gives you and your partner satisfaction or not.

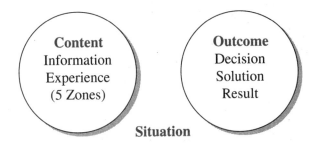

As you converse, your exchanges typically focus on content and outcome — two strong forces upon you. Gaining agreement about the significant content and the needed outcome can take on such importance, that perhaps you try to force one another to reach the agreement.

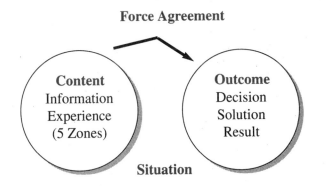

When you cannot reach agreement, pressure and stress tend to grow for both of you. At this point, it is easy to get stuck, unable to settle things satisfactorily, or you slip into a negative dance.

THE THIRD FORCE — PROCESS

Process is how you and your partner deal with the content and develop an outcome. It is the method you use for handling the situation, such as when you make a decision or plan something. The interactive interplay goes on between you as you carry on one of these activities and negotiate your differences. Process is the seemingly invisible but powerful third force that either inhibits or supports quality information and satisfying results.

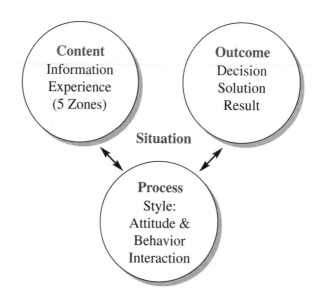

The Styles of Communication you employ, with their accompanying attitude and behaviors, contribute significantly to your process. During discussion of an important or complex situation, potential for conflict arises. At that time your interactive processes may include avoiding, persuading (which can move into forcing or manipulating), floating, compromising, or collaborating. (For more details of these types of interactions, review Chapter 3 in *Talking and Listening Together.* For Styles, see Chapter 4 in the COUPLE COMMUNICATION I book.[1])

For example, you can change the subject (Style I Small Talk) to avoid discussing in depth. When you try to persuade by giving commands or making power plays (Style II Communication), you probably produce

COMMUNICATION STYLES AND INTERACTIVE PROCESSES

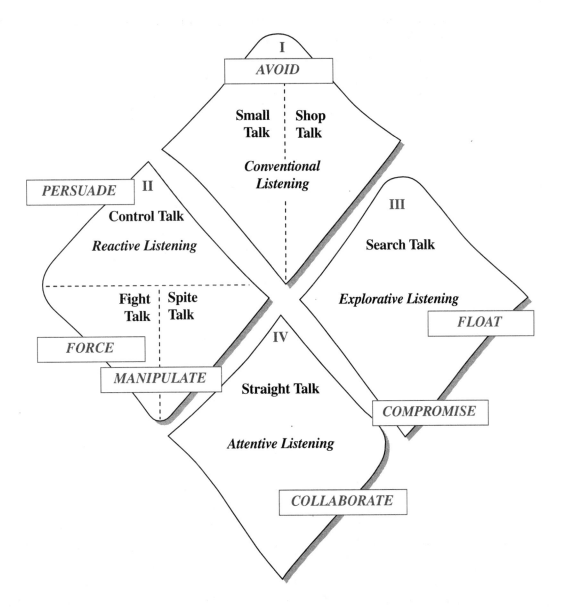

friction and stress. If you search for causes or explore through asking questions (Style III), you simply float or even compromise. If you combine Style III behaviors with disclosing your own awareness plus tuning into your partner's experience (Style IV), you can collaborate. The diagram above shows how the styles and processes interrelate.

It is important to pay attention to the process you use and alter it when you choose, since any situation holds potential for conflict regarding the content and the outcome. In fact, the process itself, in many situations, either reduces or generates conflict. Ultimately, it also influences your level of satisfaction about the entire situation.

In your interactions with one another, you may both use skills, or one may apply them while the other does not. It is also possible that neither of you uses skills. However, a skilled, caring process facilitates quality content and best-fit outcomes for both people. The skills in Styles III and IV will help you achieve understanding and build agreement.

STYLES AND SKILLS

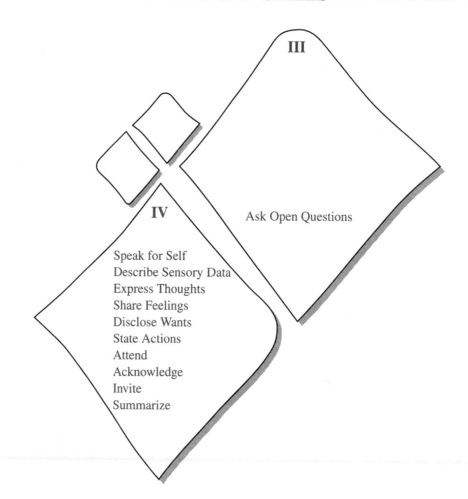

III

Ask Open Questions

IV

Speak for Self
Describe Sensory Data
Express Thoughts
Share Feelings
Disclose Wants
State Actions
Attend
Acknowledge
Invite
Summarize

IT TAKES ONE PARTNER

Even though you and your partner may both know how to use communication skills, sometimes one of you may set those skills aside, for instance, when one of you initiates a change. Then it becomes easy for the other to let the the skills go, as well. However, now that you know the skills, realize the following:

It takes only one person to influence an interaction.

You by yourself can make a difference. It is *your* choice about whether to use the skills or not, regardless of what your partner does. You choose the communication style *you* use.

This means you do not need to depend on your partner using the skills for you to apply them. Rather, you can take personal responsibility to influence your conversation positively, which is particularly important during an important or heated discussion. You, on your own, can apply your awareness and skills in a caring way.

USE YOUR FULL REPERTOIRE OF SKILLS

In your life, literally (with the mats) or figuratively, you as an individual possess 11 communication skills that you can use in any interactive situation. You can apply them in any combination and sequence. The small skills mat shows the 11 skills before you and alerts you to your choices, including the options of Check Process and Time Out. The complete set of 11 skills supports a collaborative process.

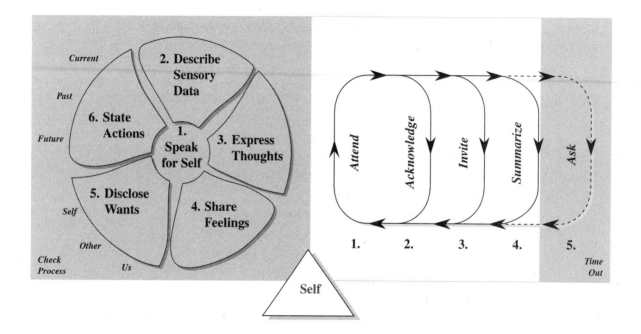

LEADING AND FOLLOWING SKILLS

In addition to considering the skills simply as talking or listening skills, another way of thinking about them is to view them as skills for leading or following the interaction.

Many interactions between you and your partner contain leading or following behaviors. Leading means talking or asking questions. Following means listening. When you lead, you attempt to direct where the conversation goes, rather than follow along with it. When you follow, you try to tune into the other person. The skills can help you do both more effectively.

Notice the two shaded areas in the diagram on the previous page. These areas highlight the leading skills. The clear area represents the following skills.

Also note that while asking open questions is considered a listening skill, it is also a leading behavior. Questions come from the asker's agenda (awareness, curiosity, or interest), and not necessarily from that of the one who is telling about or initiating something. So when you ask questions, you are influencing the direction of the conversation. This can be a useful leading behavior, or it can be sidetracking and even distracting, depending on the situation.

The four other listening skills are following skills. Their major purpose is to allow and encourage the talker to lead in any direction, in order for the listener to discover and understand the talker's experience. Most people would rather lead (talk or ask questions) than follow (listen). At the same time, most people also want to be listened to and to be understood accurately.

Advantages of Following

Allowing your partner to lead has several advantages:

- Generally you move to the core of the situation or issue faster.

- You earn the right to be heard after you have listened to your partner tell his or her story.

- Your partner likely feels pleased to have been listened to by you. This builds relationship.

During an exchange with your partner, whether or not your partner is using the skills, you always have a choice — to lead or to follow. Your effectiveness at using the skills can influence the interaction positively.

CHOICE POINTS

When you are in a serious discussion with your partner, if what you are doing in the exchange seems to be working — meaning you are connecting and things are going well — you probably feel pleased. If, on the other hand, you realize (perhaps in a split second) that what you are doing is not working — meaning that you are meeting resistance or not being heard — you are at a critical moment. You are at a choice point, a potential turning point in the interaction.

Watch Hot or Cold

How do you judge if your conversation is working or not working in any situation? One way to evaluate, besides hearing the words, is to watch your partner's hot and cold nonverbal responses.

When you were a child, you may recall playing a game called "Hot or Cold," "Hide the Thimble," or something similar. The rules were simple: Someone left the room and the other people hid an object. When the individual re-entered the room, he or she was supposed to find the hidden object based on the verbal feedback the others in the room provided.

As the seeker moved closer to the hidden object, the others called out, "Warm!" "Hot!" or (very close) "Burning up!" If the person moved away from the object, the others would say, "You're cold!" "Ice cold!" or "Freezing!"

The game was fun, and the seeker would readily find the object as long as he or she:

1. Was given accurate feedback.

2. Attended to and used the feedback.

If the seeker was given inaccurate information by others or did not attend to the feedback, the game became a frustrating random search without helpful information.

Interpersonal communication operates on a feedback system very much like playing the game "Hot or Cold." Your partner's nonverbals are the hot or cold feedback that give you clues as to whether what you are doing is working or not working in the interaction. The nonverbals suggest if your actions receive a:

- Positive (hot) response — consideration, acceptance, agreement
- Negative (cold) response — reluctance, disagreement, rejection

As you have learned to know your partner, you probably have come to recognize his or her individual subtle or not so subtle nonverbal behaviors. These include, for example, small facial changes, gestures, head movements and posture shifts. Other nonverbals include rate, pitch, volume, and tone of voice. Some nonverbals consist of even larger body gestures.

Since nonverbals are spontaneous and hard to control consciously, they often reflect emotion and operate outside the sender's awareness. These nonverbal cues from your partner serve as your interpersonal sensory data base — feedback to you.

The next time you and your partner are in an important exchange, pay attention to his or her hot and cold nonverbals and use these as your cue to alter the leading and following communication skills you employ. Also, realize that how you intend a message and how you partner interprets your action do not always match. Attending to your partner's hot and cold nonverbals can help you clarify these miscommunications.

Recognize, Stop, and Shift

When you recognize that what you are doing is not working, you are at a choice point — that of continuing your current behavior or of doing something different. If you choose to stop and shift to another behavior, you increase the possibility of turning the interaction around so that it does work. For example, if you are leading (talking or questioning), stop and shift to following (listening). If you are following (acknowledging, for instance), stop and shift to leading (such as disclosing your wants for the other person).

Besides changes of leading to following and vice versa, other stop/shifts include altering zones of the Awareness Wheel (for example, go from focusing on your feelings to giving your past behavior that has contributed to the situation).

Experiment in an interaction with your partner when things are not flowing smoothly. Change your own behavior to connect with your partner and influence the climate positively. Do not keep doing what is not working. If you do, you will keep getting the same results. Let your partner's hot and cold responses be your guide to skill use.

Stay on the Mat — Literally or Figuratively

When you hit resistance — cold responses — you may be tempted to take one of two actions. The first is to become aggressive, stepping forward off the mat attempting to force change. The second is to withdraw negatively from the situation, stepping backward off the mat. Do not do either one. Rather, keep the leading and following behaviors in mind and step sideways on the mat. Stay present and experiment with the 11 skills, engaging your partner's awareness, and expressing your own in the process.

INITIATING AND RESPONDING TO CHANGE

As you make decisions, solve problems, or plan activities, at some point, probably one of you proposes an idea or suggestion, and the other replies. This initiating and responding to change often is the type of interaction in which communication troubles occur.

It is useful to keep in mind several guidelines for handling each side of the exchange — initiating or responding. The next page contains several guidelines that will help you initiate change in a positive manner.

GUIDELINES FOR INITIATING CHANGE POSITIVELY

Any time you initiate change, you get immediate, nonverbal feedback. Partners cannot, not communicate something. Keep the guidelines below in mind to initiate the change positively.

Do:

- Pick a good time and place.

- Speak for yourself in a positive, attractive tone.

- Use any or all the skills — Straight Talk and Attentive Listening.

- Incorporate partner's interests — give wants for other.

- Summarize your understanding of your partner's responses.

- Acknowledge reluctance (a cold response).

- Invite partner to talk.

- Alternate leading and following.

- Watch hot or cold responses.

- Pursue understanding before agreement.

- Maximize choice.

Do Not:

- Violate boundaries — bring something up inappropriately in front of other people.

- Use "you" messages.

- Start with or slip into a whiney, demanding, or abrasive tone and posture (Style II behaviors).

- Criticize (Style II).

- Expect to get everything you suggest.

- Keep doing what is not working (fail to Recognize/Stop/Shift).

- Force agreement or withdraw negatively (which would be leaving the mat).

INITIATE CHANGE POSITIVELY

Instructions: Arrange your large floor mats side by side in the same way that you see the Awareness Wheel and the Listening Cycle on your small laptop mat. The Awareness Wheel will be to the left before you and the Listening Cycle to the right. Stand in front of the mats, and ask your partner to stand off the mats across from you.

Engage your partner in a conversation in which you initiate a change (propose an idea or make a suggestion). As you do so, be aware of whether you are using the leading and following skills. Step to each skill you use as you are using it. Your partner responds (off the mats) to your initiating efforts. Watch your partner's hot and cold responses to see if what you are doing is working or not working. If you recognize a cold response, stop and shift to another skill or shift from leading to following, or vice versa.

Remember, when you make decisions, solve problems, or plan activities, that either side of the exchange — initiator of or responder to an idea — can influence the interaction. You and your partner each make choices. Following are guidelines for keeping the interaction positive when you are the one responding.

GUIDELINES FOR RESPONDING TO CHANGE POSITIVELY

Your response influences the exchange. Apply the guidelines below.

Do:

- Use the listening skills to understand the proposed change:

  Attend
  Ask
  Invite
  Summarize

- Tell your partner you are desiring to understand, not necessarily to agree, if that is the case.

- Speak for yourself in response.

- Watch hot and cold nonverbals in your initiating partner as you respond.

- Say which part you would find useful to do, if any part fits.

Do Not:

- Use "you" messages.
- Start with or slip into a whiney, demanding, or abrasive tone and posture (Style II behaviors).
- Criticize (Style II).
- Keep doing what is not working (fail to Recognize/Stop/Shift).
- Withdraw negatively.

COLLABORATIVE COMMUNICATION

As a couple, you increase your capacity to handle non-routine, uncertain, or pressured situations when you both operate collaboratively. This means that you both apply all the skills to access the relevant information (content) inside each of you to help you produce satisfying outcomes. You use your process to pursue understanding and build agreements.

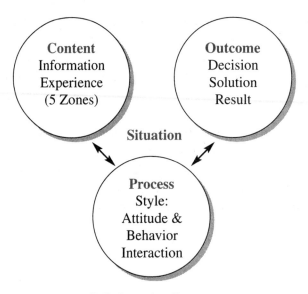

Collaborative Process
Pursues Understanding/Builds Agreement

Collaborative communication supports a dynamic, experience-based dialogue rather than a static, position-based advocacy. When you collaborate, you mutually disclose and tune into each other's data, thoughts, emotions, and interests (wants), as you discuss and generate possibilities. This combines the communication of Style III (Search Talk and Explorative Listening) and Style IV (Straight Talk and Attentive Listening). You do not simply defend and protect positions (who is right or wrong) and preconceived outcomes (shoulds), Style II communication.

Putting Collaborative Communication to Work

In COUPLE COMMUNICATION I, you learned Mapping an Issue, an eight-step structured process for resolving conflicts collaboratively. (In that process, each of you used a set of skills — either talking or listening — one set at a time, according to a particular procedure. You took turns moving from one skills mat to the other, across from one another, as you discussed the issue.)

Now with Collaborative Communication, you can also use a more free-flowing approach to deal with a variety of situations. In this more fluid option, with the Awareness Wheel and the Listening Cycle oriented side by side (on the laptop mat), each of you has the full repertoire of skills in front of you.

This means that both of you individually can be prompted by and choose from any of the skills, in any order, when you are in conversation with one another. You may use your fingers on the laptop mat if you wish, to track your skill choice, as you sit together. This arrangement allows you to carry on a natural yet skillful and productive discussion, about any situation or issue.

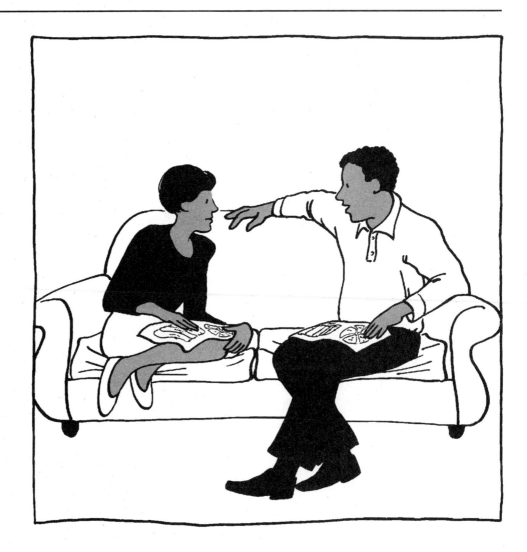

GUIDELINES FOR COMMUNICATING COLLABORATIVELY

Do:
- Count self and other.

- Choose a good time and place to talk.

- Expand awareness — start anywhere, go anywhere.

- Use all the skills, and particularly:

    Own your own actions.

    Express wants for other— partner's interests.

    Make commitments for future acton(s).

- Watch hot and cold nonverbals — what is working or not working.

- Alter leading and following (based on hot or cold responses).

- Pursue mutual understanding.

- Check process occasionally.

- Call Time Out as needed.

- Invent options for mutual benefit.

- Build agreements.

- Develop best-fit solutions.

- Seek high satisfaction with process and outcome.

- Have some fun with the process.

Do Not:
- Limit self or other awareness.

- Make conditional proposals.

- Leave the mats (literally or figuratively) to force agreement or withdraw negatively.

SKILLS FOR COLLABORATIVE COMMUNICATION

(Using Two Laptop Mats or Four Floor Mats)

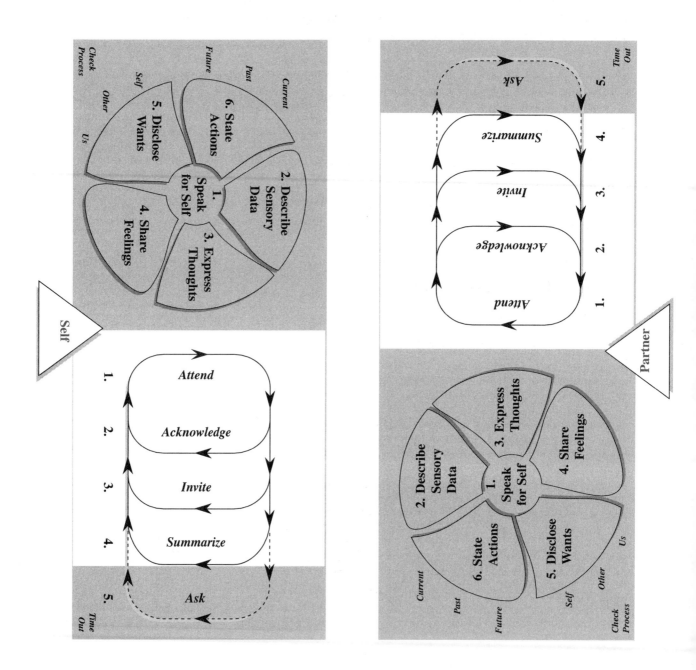

CHECKING PROCESS — ATTENDING TO THE THIRD FORCE

One of the goals of COUPLE COMMUNICATION II is to increase your ability to both participate in and observe your own interactions. These activities involve understanding and monitoring your process — your own contribution and response, as well as your partner's.

Checking process means stepping outside your conversation for a moment and "talking about your talking." This means shifting from discussing an issue or situation directly, into checking out or talking about the process of your interaction itself.

Checking Process helps you be more in charge of your conversations. It provides a vehicle to self-monitor, to self-alter, if necessary, and to self-direct your own exchanges. This tends to keep the process of your conversations mutually meaningful, efficient, productive, and satisfying.

Checking process consists of three aspects:

- Pre-Talk — How you will interact

- Now-Talk — How you are interacting

- Post Talk — How you did or have interacted

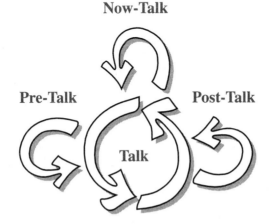

Now-Talk

Pre-Talk   **Post-Talk**

Talk

Pre-Talk

In Pre-Talk you arrange for or anticipate a discussion by setting the stage for a constructive exchange. It provides orientation for what is to follow. This includes:

- Previewing what you want to talk about — identifying the issue or situation.

- Contracting for a conversation, such as scheduling time and place.

- Setting expectations

Now-Talk

Now-Talk focuses on what is happening in the interaction at the moment: what you are immediately sensing, thinking, feeling, wanting or doing in relation to your immediate dance. Comments or questions can relate to positive feedback — what you like — or negative observations, along with suggestions or requests for change or help. Now-Talk elements include:

- Commenting on the moment, related to the way things are going process-wise, such as:

    Sharing positive feelings.

    Expressing appreciation.

    Expressing frustration.

- Noticing a change of issue.

- Commenting on effectiveness of, or lack of, skill use.

- Clarifying procedures.

- Monitoring progress.

- Giving or asking for feedback.

Post-Talk

After you have resolved an issue or finished an important conversation, the Post-Talk allows you to reflect on the event. Sometimes you do this with an eye to learning from the exchange. Post-Talk involves:

- Expressing satisfaction with either the process or the outcome, or both.

- Analyzing mishaps to change in the future.

- Commenting on what you have learned (process-wise) for the future.

- Thanking your partner for his or her contribution or help.

- Clearing the air (such as apologizing for unpleasant behavior).

- Celebrating results.

By anticipating, altering, and reviewing actions at the process level, you can stay, or get back on track more easily. In addition to preventing or helping repair misunderstandings, checking process lets you savor your exchanges, as well.

LIST OF SITUATIONS/ISSUES

Date _____

Instructions:

1. Spend a few minutes individually thinking about situations or issues that are important for you and your partner at this time. Perhaps you have a decision to make, a problem to solve, an activity to plan, or several options requiring you to set priorities. Write down the topics.

2. Share these with your partner.

SITUATION FOR COLLABORATIVE COMMUNICATION

Instructions:

1. Choose one of the situations/issues which you and your partner listed on your individual worksheets on the previous page to discuss following the directions given in this exercise.

2. Prepare yourselves. In a learning/coaching context, use four large mats, so an instructor or other couple can coach you. Face one another, each with two floor mats in front of you. For each, place the Awareness Wheel mat on the left and the Listening Cycle on the right in front of you. (If you are on your own, both of you use the small laptop mats.) See page 56 for the layout. Now you both have all the skills from which to choose.

3. Discuss the situation, stepping from skill to skill on the mat as you each use the skills. (Or use your fingers on the small mat to track and prompt yourself.) Keep the leading and following behaviors in mind. If appropriate, Check Process along the way by doing Now-Talk.

   Coaches: Observe and coach on the following:

   - Use of the skills
   - Mix of leading and following skills
   - Hot and cold nonverbals
   - Disclosure of wants for other
   - Statements of past, current, and future actions

4. Do Post-Talk. Afterward, talk about how your use of skills in this prompted yet free-style way influenced the quality of the content and the outcome of your situation.

A COLLABORATIVE OPERATING SYSTEM FOR THRIVING COUPLES

When you and your partner choose to communicate collaboratively, the process itself becomes your "common operating system" — way of relating that permeates your life together. Using the same system as one another, you possess the capacity to create constructive exchanges, whether you engage challenging situations or just enjoy each other on a daily basis.

As you heighten your ability to attend well to the processes you use — to refine and continue to develop your skills inside your partnership — you honor one another and make a positive impact upon your relationship.

PARTNER DISCUSSIONS

Collaborative Communication

Together with your partner, pick a new situation in which you wish to:

- Make a decision
- Solve a problem
- Plan an activity
- Set some priorities

Use your small laptop mats to prompt your skills, keeping the leading and following behaviors in mind. Check process, as necessary with Now-Talk.

Afterwards, use Post-Talk to process the conversation.

Responding to Change

Set up a practice opportunity in which you request your partner to initiate a change with you, and you respond to your partner. Place your small skills mat in front of you. Ask your partner *not* to use his or her mat.

Apply the leading or following skills. Point to each skill you use, as you are using it on your laptop mat. Watch your partner's hot and cold nonverbals to see if what you are doing is working or not working. If you recognize a cold nonverbal behavior, stop and shift to another skill or move from leading to following, or visa versa.

Issue of Conflict

As partners, take an issue of conflict and with mutually caring attitudes, use your laptop skills mats to help you maintain a collaborative process to discuss and resolve the difference.

Asking Your Partner for Change

1. Use a sheet from your Awareness Wheel pad, and expand your awareness about something you would like your partner, or the two of you together, to change.

2. After you complete your Wheel, think about your partner and how he or she could best hear your request. Number the zones of your Wheel from 1 to 5 in an order that you think would make it easiest for your partner to hear and understand your request.

3. Pick a good time and place to approach your partner. Ask if he or she would first listen to understand your request (Pre-Talk).

4. Speak for yourself and briefly present your Wheel following the sequence in Step 2.

5. Invite your partner to respond.

6. Maintain a skilled, collaborative process to negotiate the change, if necessary.

OTHER ACTIVITIES

Individual Debriefing

Review a conversation you have had with your partner that did not go well. Use your laptop mat to see what you could have done differently to have made the conversation more collaborative. Focus on your own behavior and not your partner's.

"Let Your Fingers Do the Walking"

Put the laptop skills mat in front of your phone (at home or work). Use the mat to track your process and to practice your talking and listening skills, as you talk on the phone with people other than your partner. In addition to extending your use of the skills to other people, this will help you apply the skills with your partner more naturally and effectively.

MANAGING
MY ANGER

Changing Unhealthy
into Healthy Expressions

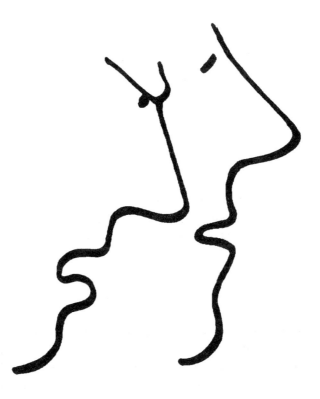

3

Managing My Anger

Nothing can put you in a negative climate faster than your anger. Feeling angry alters your body chemistry, signals to others the need to defend or move away, and makes the atmosphere tense and uncomfortable — even before you ever open your mouth. The impact to yourself, as well as to anyone else around, is strong, often in ways that you do not want. Anger that is expressed in unhealthy ways and that gets out of hand can harm yourself and your partner, and it has potential for destroying your relationship.

Managing your anger allows you to take this emotion, when it arises in you, and make constructive changes, which are caring for yourself and others involved, in the situation or your life. When you manage your anger, you enjoy more satisfying relationships, a healthier, happier life, and an increased sense of well-being. Your endeavors are more productive, as well.

You make choices that can result in your anger controlling you or you managing your anger. To determine choice points, it is helpful to understand about anger itself — what is involved in this emotion, various expressions of it, and strategies for dealing with it.

Anger — A Powerful Feeling

Anger, as any other emotion, is your spontaneous physiological response to your interpretation of sensory data. It is a biological reaction that happens within you, and it registers in your body. When you take in sensory data, make meaning of a situation, and respond in anger, your emotion happens instantaneously. For example, the data may or may not match your beliefs, expectations, or desires at the time. The stronger your beliefs, expectations, or desires about something, the stronger the resulting anger about it, if that is your emotional response.

Even though the feeling of anger occurs without your immediate control, once you gain awareness of it, your anger loses its power over you. As you recognize and acknowledge to yourself the anger, you can learn ways to manage yourself and express it appropriately.

COMPONENTS OF ANGER

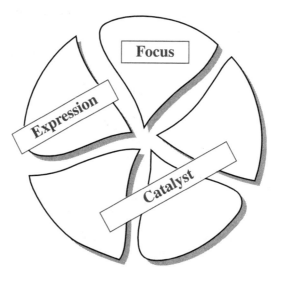

The specific components of anger include the focus, the catalyst, and the expression of this emotion. You can understand the components more readily by seeing how they fit particular zones of the Awareness Wheel.

FOCUS

The focus of your anger — who or what you are angry at — refers to three elements in the *sensory data* zone of the Awareness Wheel. These include:

A Person

This is someone who stands in your way or acts in a manner you believe discounts, offends, or violates you. For example, your partner could be late for an occasion that is very important for you, even though you had talked about this together ahead of time.

An Event

This could be information, an occurrence of some sort, a natural disaster, or an accident. For instance, you hear that possible layoffs will occur at your company just after you have signed a contract to move to a new home.

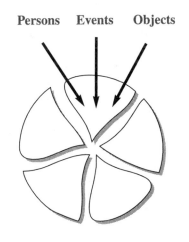

Persons   Events   Objects

An Object

This refers to something such as a broken piece of equipment. For instance, your car battery is dead as you get ready to leave for the airport.

CATALYST

The catalyst — what you bring to the situation — is the stimulating force for your anger. It comes from within yourself, from one or a combination of the thought, feeling, or want zones of your Awareness Wheel. A catalyst can be:

Your Thoughts

You hold expectations about something that go unfulfilled. Or, needs you believe are important to you have not been met. For example, on a holiday, you expect family members to gather, and your partner, who is not particularly comfortable with your family, makes arrangements for you both to get together with friends instead.

Or, you interpret that your personal worth or dignity is demeaned or undermined. This can range from a casual put down to a full-blown insult to you as a person. You think you are being devalued, unloved, or treated as unimportant. Any of these thoughts can give rise to your anger.

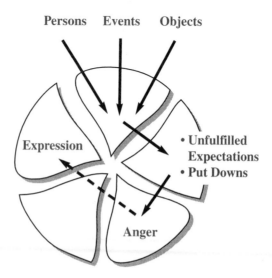

Your Feelings

You experience the emotion of fear about the threat of danger, vulnerability, or loss. While it is your interpretation (a thought) about a threat, the emotion is fear, and the fear turns into anger. Sometimes it happens so fast you may not even recognize the fear behind it. For instance, in the example given before in which layoffs might occur at your company just after you have signed a contract for a new home, you may actually fear great financial loss or economic hardships. The fear gets covered by the anger.

Or, you are very sad about something disappointing that happens, and the sadness goes to anger. The change of the emotion of fear or sadness into anger may occur instantaneously, and you may be unaware and jump over experiencing the underlying feeling of fear or sadness.

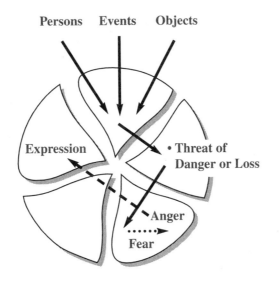

Your Wants

When you are blocked in gaining something you desire, you become angry. If a goal you are aiming for is thwarted or interference occurs, the emotion that arises in you is anger. In these instances, it is your interpretation that the focus of your anger is preventing you from experiencing your wants.

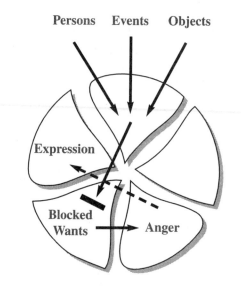

EXPRESSION

The way you express your anger fits into the action zone of the Awareness Wheel, and how you express it may be unhealthy or healthy for you and your relationships. Each type of expression impacts yourself and others. Even if the focus is not your partner, how you handle your anger can affect your relationship.

It is useful to view various expressions of anger — whether unhealthy or healthy —in terms of how your energy is channeled and translated into your talking or other behavior. Usually people develop a major way of expressing anger, regardless of what the focus or catalyst is. Notice if one of these expressions is what you typically do.

UNHEALTHY EXPRESSIONS

Venting

If you vent, you spew your energy directly and forcefully at the focus of your anger, with much Fight Talk and other attacking behaviors. Your negative energy rushes out in torrents. It floods anything or anyone with less power than your anger.

When the focus of your anger is another person, your venting is typically hurtful to that person, and often damaging to your relationship. Over time, the venting of anger generally increases more readily, with the focus and catalyst combining very quickly to release destructive bursts. Evidence indicates that excessive venting correlates with more subsequent aggression.[1]

The impact of venting anger is harmful to you, at least long-term, even though short-term, it may appear to bring you benefits. For example, you can experience consequences to your health, such as increased risk of heart disease.[2]

Also, venting often destroys intimacy, even with people who are not the focus of the anger, as others back away for their own protection.

> Physical violence in any form — hurtful touching, pushing, hitting, etc. — is an unhealthy expression of anger taken to extreme. This is never acceptable.

Displacing

When you displace your anger, you do not direct it at the actual focus of your anger. Rather you aim it at somebody or something else. Typically that someone else holds less power than you or the focus itself, at least in your estimation. As a result, you misdirect your anger more freely. For example, you may be angry at a manager at work, and come home and yell at or hit your dog, child, or spouse.

When it comes out, your behavior towards that something else may be much the same as in venting. Sometimes, because a time lag may have occurred between the situation in focus, the catalyst may have gained force, making the expression stronger and possibly more aggressive than it might originally have been.

The impact of displaced anger is harmful to you, with consequences for you similar to those of venting. The impact to the actual focus may be minimal or nil, at least directly. However, the impact can be hurtful or even devastating to the one who actually receives the displaced behavior. Displaced anger can lower the trust of anyone on the receiving end and undermine any type of positive climate being developed. It can damage relationships with people close to you, and this is especially sad, because the anger is really at someone or something else.

Leaking

If you express your anger this way, it is as though you leak your energy from cracks, and the seepage reaches the focus of your anger indirectly. You use Spite Talk or mixed messages, or you take covert, negative retaliatory actions that eventually affect the focus.

Similar to anything that leaks, your anger can make a mess for whatever surrounds you and the focus. Besides doing some type of apparent damage to the specific focus, you eventually contaminate others, too, before you are finished. For example, you are angry at your partner for deciding, without your input, that the whole family will go camping at a particular spot for a vacation, so you intentionally neglect to let your partner know about the deadline for reservations at the popular area until it is too late. When the trip does not work out, the rest of the family, besides your partner, is disappointed and unhappy.

The anger you leak registers in your body, affecting your physiology negatively. Over time, with this expression of anger, your health will be affected. Also, because unintended areas of harm often occur from leaking your anger, something could return to hurt you in ways you have not anticipated. For instance, you make a false or exaggerated statement inappropriately about the focus of your anger to a third party at work. Your remarks are passed along, and while they may have temporarily hurt the focus, they also come back to harm you when you are passed over for a promotion.

Holding and Absorbing

When you hold your angry energy in, you withdraw from the focus of it. You review inwardly the sensory data from the focus and replay in various ways the catalytic parts. You do not take action, at least for a time, but absorb the negativity. You use Small and Shop Talk or perhaps "No Talk" to the focus. During this time, the catalysts can build, fester, or finally dissipate.

The impact can be very strong to you, with this form of expression. You can get toxic, and become ill or depressed. Your immune system is lowered. Feelings other than anger can be blocked, as you put up a wall between yourself and the focus. Over time, the impact to you is definitely hurtful physically and emotionally.[3]

With this expression, the impact to the focus of your anger is less certain. The person who is the focus probably receives confusing messages from you, and as time passes, may in turn withdraw from you as well.

When pent up angry energy eventually comes out, it may explode excessively, far out of proportion to the data to which the catalyst in you reacted. When it stays inside, it eats away at you.

HEALTHY EXPRESSIONS

Acting Constructively

When you act constructively to deal with your anger, you use any of a variety of actions that are in alignment and congruent with your awareness. The expression is something you manage. You take care of yourself, not letting the anger damage yourself physically, emotionally or hurt your relationships. In addition, your actions take into account and show care for the focus of the anger, whatever or whoever that is.

The impact of your expression is helpful, creating positive change for the situation. When it involves a relationship, it often brings the relationship to a new level of understanding and respect. Your expression gives you freedom in your life and a freedom in your relationships as well. It releases energy for other areas of living, which is better for your health and well-being.

Staying on the Mat

When you experience anger, think of your skills mats. Literally or figuratively, either you stay on the mats or you leave the mats to express your anger.

When you *act aggressively,* you step off the mat toward the focus of your anger, directing, pressing, demanding, blaming, threatening or attacking. When you *act passively,* you step off the mat backwards, absorbing, suppressing, and retaining the anger — or you distance yourself by running from the focus of your anger. When you *act indirectly,* you step off to the side, or operate under the table, so to speak, mixing both passive and aggressive behaviors.

To act congruently, you stay on the mats, mustering your full awareness, personal presence, and communication skills to deal constructively with the focus of your anger.

How do you typically handle your anger? Look at the diagram on the next page, and consider your usual form of expressing your anger.

WAYS OF EXPRESSING ANGER

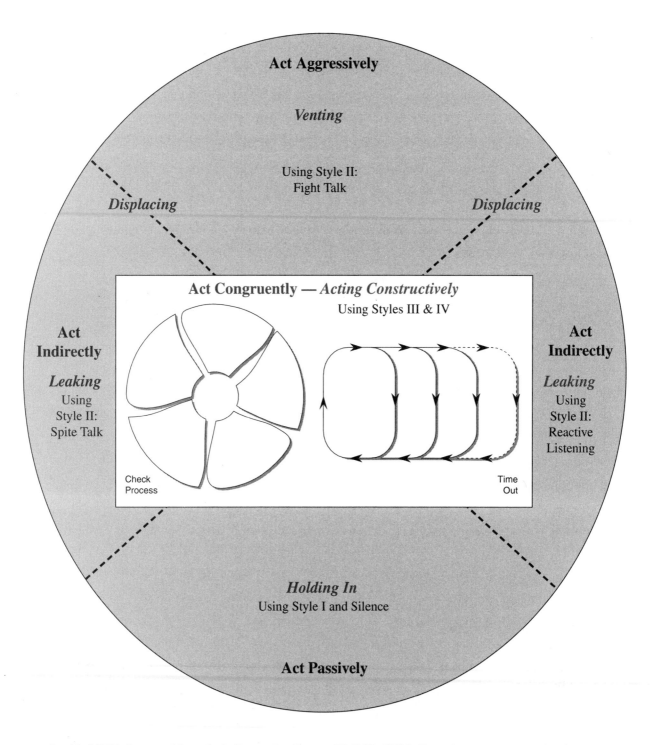

Act Aggressively

Venting

Using Style II:
Fight Talk

Displacing   *Displacing*

Act Congruently — *Acting Constructively*
Using Styles III & IV

**Act
Indirectly**   **Act
Indirectly**

Leaking   *Leaking*
Using   Using
Style II: Style II:
Spite Talk   Reactive
                                                       Listening

Check
Process   Time
                                                       Out

Holding In
Using Style I and Silence

Act Passively

FOCUS, CATALYST, EXPRESSION, AND IMPACT OF MY UNHEALTHY ANGER

Instructions: Think of a situation in which you became angry at a person, event, or object and your expression was unhealthy. (Try to choose something that might typify what you usually do.)

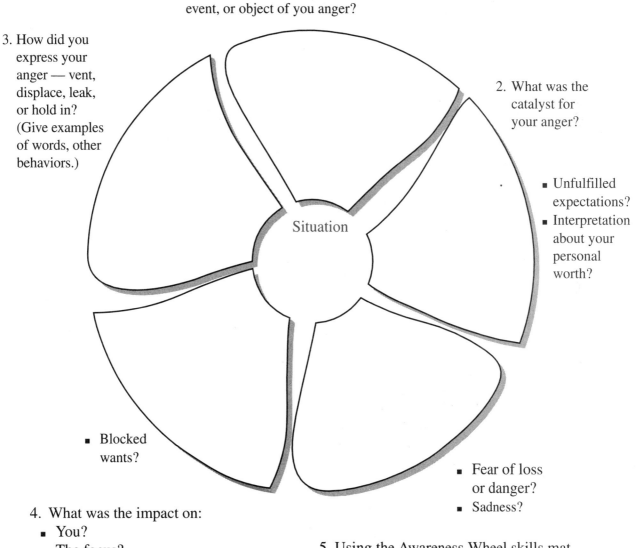

1. What was the specific target: person, event, or object of you anger?

2. What was the catalyst for your anger?
   - Unfulfilled expectations?
   - Interpretation about your personal worth?
   - Fear of loss or danger?
   - Sadness?
   - Blocked wants?

3. How did you express your anger — vent, displace, leak, or hold in? (Give examples of words, other behaviors.)

4. What was the impact on:
   - You?
   - The focus?
   - Others around?

5. Using the Awareness Wheel skills mat, tell your partner about your experience of your unhealthy expression of anger.

Situation

MANAGING MY ANGER

In managing anger, you begin with yourself. You first look at yourself and care about yourself. You figure out what is going on and what is making you angry. You try to understand yourself, the situation, and if there is another person, understand the other person. Then you employ caring behavior toward anyone involved. In other words, you manage the way you process your anger.

HOW TO MANAGE MY ANGER

To manage your own anger means that you take three major steps to deal with your experience. An easy way to remember them is to call them the RCA steps. Here is a quick overview, and then each step is described in more detail.

R: Recognize and Rebalance

To take this step, you recognize cues to anger, and you rebalance yourself physically.

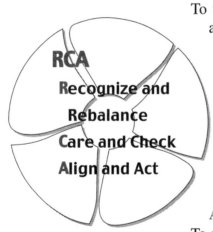

C: Care and Check

To carry out this step, you remind yourself to care about yourself and the other person, and you check your awareness of the situation.

A: Align and Act

To do this, you align your awareness and take actions constructive for the situation.

STEP 1: RECOGNIZE AND REBALANCE

In this two-part step, recognize cues to your anger and rebalance yourself physically.

Recognize Cues:

A first part of managing anger is to recognize its appearance as it is occurring. You can notice cues of anger — signals in your own body, your specific styles of communication or mixed messages, and your attitude.

Cues in Your Body

Your body gives physiological signals of anger. When the catalyst in you (your interpretation, fear, or blocked want) brings anger for the sensory data you experience, you have a physiological reaction. Most typically the reaction includes:

- Your upper body — face, neck, shoulders, and chest — tightens and your muscles tense.

- Your breathing tends to be more rapid, shallow, and possibly forced.

- Your heart rate increases.

- Your vision and hearing narrow or become fixed. You see and hear less.

- Certain chemicals (from the adrenal gland) in the the body increase. An adrenaline rush occurs, which numbs your body to pain and temporarily increases your physical strength.

Physical arousal is inversely related to your ability to think effectively. However, once you become aware of any of these physiological cues, you can learn to recognize them in yourself, and when you do, take actions to manage yourself better.

Cues in Your Styles of Communication

In anger, if you are like many people, you use Style II communication: Control, Fight, or Spite Talk and Reactive Listening. You talk too much, and do not listen, or you may also use "No Talk," in angry silence. Your tone of voice, general demeanor, and choice of words signal the anger and tension, whether it is directly aggressive or passively punitive. You may also use mixed messages, which include an undercurrent of Style II combined with any other style. The overall message is contradictory or unclear, and the negative aspect of the message registers the strongest impact. For example,

> "I appreciate your stopping for take-out on your way home (Straight Talk), but it took you forever and nobody's hungry now" (Fight or Spite Talk, depending on tone).

Too much use of Style II, and sometimes any use of Style II, signals anger. It can heat up an interaction, particularly when an issue is involved. Recognizing your use of this style, whether by itself or combined with another style to make a mixed message, helps alert you to angry feelings you are experiencing and the need to take notice of and deal with them in a productive way.

Cues in Your Attitude

In anger, your attitude toward the focus most typically is uncaring, at least in the short term. For the moment, you do not take the focus into account, value who or what it is, or consider the situation from any perspective other than your own. You assume that you count and the focus does not. You believe that your concern far outweighs the significance of any concern that the focus of your anger has.

Ironically, your attitude toward yourself may be uncaring, too, by overlooking, denying, or allowing consequences to self that come from expressing your anger in an unhealthy way. For example, it may be hard on you physically. It could be embarrassing ultimately or have untoward repercussions later on (for instance, it could ruin an important family gathering or eliminate you from an opportunity at work).

Being aware of your attitude toward another or yourself can be a signal to you that you are feeling anger, and that it is time to do something to handle it productively and effectively.

Any one of the cues, whether in your body, your style of communication or your attitude, can let you know you are angry and need to manage yourself. This does not require that you are aware of all three types of cues at once; rather, it is helpful to notice whichever one or combination is a cue to you, and let that be a signal for you to rebalance yourself.

Rebalance Yourself

As soon as you recognize that you are angry or upset, at that moment rebalance yourself by consciously taking a deep, relaxing breath. (Be careful that your breath is not taken so loudly that your partner or others around you think your anger is escalating.)

The effect will be to lessen muscle tension in the upper body, reduce your heart rate, and generally calm your physiology (a caring act for yourself). This change in your breathing and presence sends more oxygen to your brain, increasing your capacity to think clearly, in order to cope with the situation. When you are balanced, you are in an alert yet relaxed state, and you are more able to care about others, as well.

How to Rebalance:

The easiest way to learn how to rebalance yourself is to:

1. Take a deep breath through your nose, with your mouth closed. Notice how, when you breathe with your mouth closed, you breathe diaphragmatically and more deeply. As you take a relaxing breath, your body tension shifts downward. Your body settles and rebalances itself naturally. Deep, relaxed breathing releases tension in your upper body and helps reconfigure your physiology.

2. As an alternative way to learn how to rebalance yourself, you can use one hand to press gently into your abdomen at the point about one-and-a-half inches below your navel. Let your upper-body muscles relax as you rebalance yourself around this physical mid-point. From this relaxed yet dynamic point of balance, you can exert minimum effort for maximum results.

With practice you can learn to rebalance yourself immediately in any position — standing, sitting, or lying down — by taking a deep, relaxing breath or by releasing any muscle tension as you settle lower into your body, regaining full presence.

With the rebalancing, your upper body muscle-tension relaxes, and the nonverbals you project undergo change (softening). Also the style of your communication is less harsh, and these alterations create the ability for you to notice your awareness, which in turn increases your choices in the situation.

STEP 2: CARE AND CHECK

Remind yourself to care about yourself and the other person, and check your awareness of the situation.

Care About Self and Other

To care for yourself and the other person(s) involved requires the recognition that what you are doing is hurting or discounting yourself, the other person, or both of you.The actual process means you ask yourself some questions: "Am I caring about myself and the other? Is this helping the situation or not?" If your answer is, "No," then you must do the next part intentionally and consciously.

That part is to say to yourself, "I care about (value and respect) myself and this person." Saying (to yourself) the message about caring can be an important turning point. It will allow you to feel more compassionate, even though it can be a difficult step when you are really angry and do not want to care.

Asking the questions and making statements set an attitudinal readiness to stop your current behavior and shift it to doing something more helpful for the situation.

Check Awareness

The natural thing do when you feel angry is to lock onto the sensory data — the focus of your anger — and blame him, her, or it for your woes. A typical statement goes, "You" or "It makes me angry!" This suggests the other person or event is in control of you, and thus determines your response. Your belief indicates that you simply operate at the mercy of the focus, and therefore act as though you have no choice in the situation.

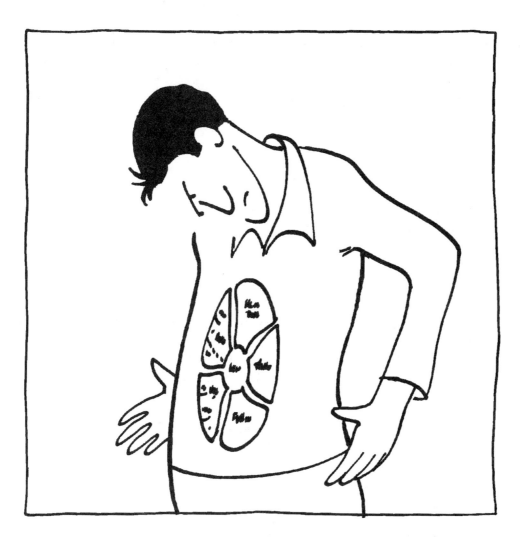

Since you believe the focus is to blame, you can justify to yourself an unhealthy expression of anger, even retaliation. Giving such power to the external focus says in effect, "I am not in control of myself." This kind of thinking lacks personal accountability or responsibility and can keep you angry and unable to deal with it constructively.

Awareness of both the outside and the inside world is important. To check awareness, discover what is really going on that is making you upset. Do an immediate check of any or all parts of your Awareness Wheel. Pay special attention to your thoughts, deeper feelings, or wants. One of these three parts of your experience has been the catalyst for your anger. For example:

- Your thoughts: Do you think you are being discounted, demeaned, or offended in some way?

- Your feelings: Do you fear some form of loss? What is hurtful or disappointing to you?

- Your wants: Are you experiencing thwarted desires or wishes?

Your awareness can range from low to high about the:

- Focus — your sensory data

- Catalyst — your thoughts, feelings, or wants

- Expression — your actions

The lower your awareness of any of these parts of your experience, the less likely you are able to take steps that are healthy for you and your relationships when anger arises in you. The higher your awareness, the more able you are to make productive and wise choices about how you express your anger. By looking inside and drawing on your internal resources, you can create congruent choices for dealing effectively with this powerful emotion. Remember, self-awareness is the foundation for choosing appropriate actions to express your anger constructively.

STEP 3: ALIGN AND ACT

Take actions that will be constructive for the situation. Choose what you say and do with your anger in a way that is in harmony (alignment) with all parts of your Wheel, including the best interests (wants) for you, for your partner or other person, and for the particular circumstances. This is acting congruently. Several kinds of actions are possible.

Speak Your Anger

In this situation, you use Straight Talk to disclose your emotion and your experiences that have given rise to it. This means you link other parts of your Wheel in a straightforward way.

Shift Your Lead/Follow Dance

Recall that in a discussion, you are either leading (talking or asking questions) or following (listening). The communication skills help you do both of these effectively. When you are feeling angry, change your dance. Some examples include:

- If you are talking rapidly (and what you are doing is not working), shift first to inviting the other person to talk and then to acknowledging that person.

- If you are telling about your angry feeling (and it is not getting you a response you like), shift to giving a want for the other person.

Keep in mind that you do not need to depend on the other person to be using the skills. You make the choice to apply them or not yourself.

Shift Your Style of Communication

In anger, often the style of communication you use can damage the situation even more, or on the other hand, can help move it to a more constructive level. For example:

- If you are using Spite Talk (and you are symbolically "off the mat"), shift to asking a question (Explorative Listening) about what the other person wants for himself or herself in the situation.

- If you are using Fight Talk (symbolically "off the mat"), shift to Straight Talk. (For instance, tell the other person your own past behavior that might have contributed to the situation.)

Do Something Differently

Change your own behavior that could be feeding the catalyst for your anger. For example:

- Stop laughing at a joke that demeans you or someone else.

- Stop participating in a certain activity.

- Decide to avoid the focus, if possible, in the future, and make arrangements to do so.

In any of these actions, you do not necessarily have to disclose to the person (focus of your anger) or anyone else your awareness of what is going on, for which you are angry. Disclosure is a separate choice from being aware and taking action. In this situation, choose to act differently.

Take a Time Out

If you are too aroused with or mired in your angry emotion and cannot act in a constructive, caring way at the moment, take a Time Out. Do this when you are:

Overwhelmed

You are too upset immediately to act congruently and appropriately. Sometimes your feelings of anger overwhelm you, and you are too flooded at the moment to act responsibly. Simply recognize your angry state and call Time Out so you can calm your physiology, in order to reflect deeper on the situation later.

Preoccupied

You are too preoccupied with anger to function well at home or work, and the situation keeps recycling inside of you. Your anger continues unabated and unresolved. It does not go away, and you find yourself mentally and emotionally preoccupied with the unsettling situation. You keep recalling the focus person, event, or object and the specific data and thoughts that upset you. In short, you are stuck in a reoccurring, possibly intensifying, cycle of anger.

Look on page 93 for suggestions about what to do during your Time Out.

You Can Choose

Even though you feel angry, you are still responsible for your own actions. You can do something that makes a constructive impact on the situation.

OTHER SUGGESTIONS FOR ACTING CONSTRUCTIVELY

If you act predominately as someone who vents, displaces, leaks, or holds in, you may want to create your own strategy for shifting to healthier expressions of anger. Consider the following suggestions for helping you customize your own healthy expressions, depending on what is typical for you.

SUGGESTIONS FOR MANAGING VENTING

- Move away, disengage from the focus of your anger temporarily until you cool down. Take a Time Out.

- Vow not to become abusive physically, verbally, or emotionally to yourself or others.

- Use an appropriate physical way to calm yourself from the adrenaline build up (exercise, go for a walk, etcetera), because thinking clearly is not possible at the point of anger.

- Do something self-soothing. For example, take a hot shower, visualize a pleasant experience or situation, pray, play a sport, or spend time with your hobby.

- Do not drive your car when you are really angry.

- Look deeper at the impacts of venting on yourself, as well as on the focus. Ask yourself whether venting really pays off for you in the long run.

- Expand your awareness about the real catalyst of your anger and make a congruent action plan when you have calmed down.

These actions will keep you from reacting rashly and regretfully.

SUGGESTIONS FOR MANAGING DISPLACING

- Go away from anyone upon whom you have displaced your anger before. Since you are in a habit of expressing your anger in the place you consider safe, once you recognize your angry feeling, stay or go to another place where you can first let go of the adrenaline build-up appropriately.

- Expand your awareness about the real focus and catalyst for your anger. Also do this away from anyone or anything upon which you have displaced your anger in the past.

- Make an action plan to deal congruently with the actual focus and catalyst.

- Find a way to reduce tension, again in an appropriate way, on a regular basis.

SUGGESTIONS FOR MANAGING LEAKING

- Recognize your indirect, spiteful comments or actions. Own your behavior.

- Expand your awareness about the focus, catalyst, and usual way you express your anger.

- Look deeper at the impacts to yourself, as well as to others besides the focus of your unhealthy expression of anger.

- Consider what has prevented you from expressing your anger directly to the focus, and make a plan that will help you deal with it in a straightforward, congruent, caring way or that will help you release it.

SUGGESTIONS FOR MANAGING HOLDING IN

- Talk to someone right away about your angry feeling. Tell him or her where you are in the process of dealing with it. For example, say you need to sort things out, if you are too confused to think clearly.

- Then, by yourself if necessary, expand your awareness.

- Make a plan, which includes addressing the anger fairly soon with another person, in a congruent and straightforward way. The other person could be the focus of your anger, if this is a close relationship, or it could be a trusted resource person, whom you believe to be supportive and helpful.

Whatever Strategy You Use ...

When you are in the habit of expressing anger in an unhealthy way, to make a change or shift requires an act of will. It means you put legs to your desire for the longer-term positive payoff (physically, emotionally, and in relationship) for yourself and that of your partner. Begin with one action. The shift may take courage and, at first, could be difficult to do. However, unless you do take a different course of action, you and others around will continue to experience the same negative climate that your anger produces.

STRATEGY FOR MANAGING MY ANGER

Instructions: Drawing from the ideas presented on the previous pages and from experiences of expressing your anger, outline what you can do in the future to manage your anger more constructively.

1. Circle your major unhealthy expression of anger: venting, displacing, leading, or holding in.

2. Imagine a situation in which you become angry. (This could be the situation you described earlier, on page 79, or a new situation.) Briefly write what the situation is.

3. How can you:

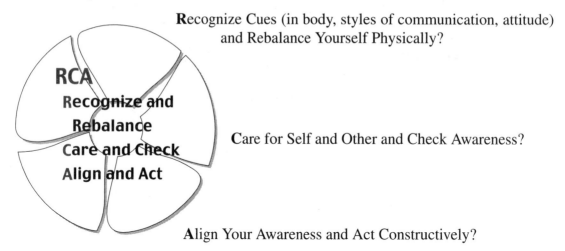

Recognize Cues (in body, styles of communication, attitude) and Rebalance Yourself Physically?

Care for Self and Other and Check Awareness?

Align Your Awareness and Act Constructively?

4. Next, imagine yourself putting your strategy into practice.

5. Share your strategy with your partner.

TIME OUT

A Time Out allows you to disengage temporarily, so that when you do move forward again, your expression will be healthy. When you take a Time Out, use the following three steps to deal with your anger. An easy way to remember them is to call them the REM steps. Here is a quick overview before each step is described in more detail.

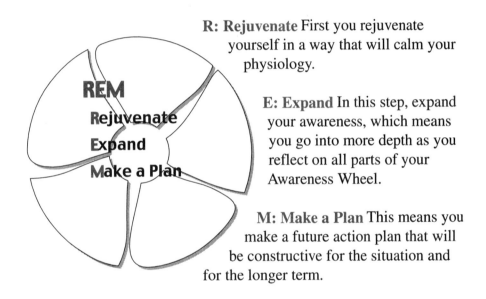

R: Rejuvenate First you rejuvenate yourself in a way that will calm your physiology.

E: Expand In this step, expand your awareness, which means you go into more depth as you reflect on all parts of your Awareness Wheel.

M: Make a Plan This means you make a future action plan that will be constructive for the situation and for the longer term.

STEP 1: REJUVENATE YOUR PHYSIOLOGY

Remember that your body has secreted chemicals that have temporarily changed your physiology. Your heart may be beating so fast (above 95 beats per minute) that it is difficult to think rationally. While your physical strength increases, your thinking can blur. Options that help you rejuvenate your physiology include to:

- Do some form of non-violent physical exercise.[4] This can be very important in managing your feelings. If physical exertion occurs during the adrenaline increase, then endorphins go into the blood and bring a sense of pleasure or euphoria, even if the emotional pain persists. An inappropriate physical exertion during anger (such as throwing something or hitting someone) could cause the desire for repetition of the behavior that brought the sense of euphoria and lead to an addiction to anger. It is better to use an appropriate lifestyle type of exercise.

- Use other calming, positive activities for you, such as praying, meditating, or listening to music. Allow something to bring your body chemistry back into balance. Of course, breathing and rebalancing intentionally for a period of time also works.

- At some point, after the increase of the chemicals from the adrenal gland, fatigue takes over. Realize this, and then do more restful activity. Without this, your resistance is lowered, and you are more susceptible to illness.

STEP 2: EXPAND YOUR AWARENESS

The goal of expanding your awareness is to understand more fully what is behind your anger. Perhaps you are experiencing something at a deeper level, just outside your immediate awareness. In your Time Out, reflect systematically. Broaden or go into more depth with your awareness about what you are experiencing.

As you reflect, use your Awareness Wheel. Be completely honest with yourself about the catalysts (thoughts, feelings, or wants) that have triggered your anger. Look at your past or current actions that may have contributed to the situation at hand, and reexamine the data.

In using your Awareness Wheel, you can

- Do so mentally. (Picture the Awareness Wheel in your mind, and reflect on each part.)

- Write on your Awareness Wheel pad, which is part of your COUPLE COMMUNICATION II packet.

- Take out a skills mat.

Your own personal preference determines the best way to do this. The important thing is to focus on each zone of the Wheel, in any order, a number of times to gain the widest understanding of your experience.

When you are away from the situation in which the anger arose in you initially, you can get a better perspective. This will give you more degrees of freedom to act when you do ultimately return.

Ask Yourself Questions

Asking yourself questions in each zone of the Wheel can help you expand your awareness of what is really going on inside you, when you are feeling angry. Consider the sample questions in the various zones.

Past or Current Actions

- What was my behavior prior to the situation?
- What, if anything, did I do to contribute to the situation?
- How have I acted thus far, in response to the focus of my anger?

Sensory Data (Regarding Focus)

- What did I see and hear?
- What have others reported about the experience?
- When, if at any other time, have I seen or heard this before?
- What other data relates to this situation?

Thoughts (Catalyst)

- What are my beliefs about this?

- How do I interpret what happened?

- What are my expectations/assumptions?

    - How important is this to me?

    - What is going on from the perspective of the focus (perhaps in that person's Wheel, if the focus is a person)?

    - How is this situation impacting me?

    - Who else is affected, and how so?

    - What deeper, more significant underlying issue does this represent?

- What am I defending or protecting? (Caution: Avoid the tendency simply to justify and defend your actions, which only reinforces your anger and keeps you stuck.)

- What am I learning from this situation?

- What, if anything, is the humor or irony in the situation?

Feelings (Catalyst)

- What other feelings do I hold? Other possibilities include:

    Fear

    Disgust

    Sadness

    Guilt or Shame

Sometimes what is experienced initially as anger may also involve feelings that are often more difficult to recognize, such as resentment or jealously.

- What, if anything am I afraid to lose?

Wants (Catalyst)

For Self

- What are my wants for myself in the situation?

- Which of these are short-term, and which are long-term?

- Do I have conflicting, incompatible wants? If so, which are they, and how do they conflict with one another?

For Other(s)

- What positively do I want for my partner or other person(s) with whom I am angry (if indeed it is a person)?

When you are really angry with someone, it is very difficult to think about the other's interests — what you want for him or her positively. However, without genuinely considering positive wants for the other person, you run the risk of never being able to move beyond your angry feelings. This is foundational for reaching a best-fit solution for everyone involved.

For Us (If the focus is someone in a close relationship)

- What do I want positively for us, short-term and long-term?

- What do I desire for our system as a whole?

Generate Options (Thoughts)

At this point, generate possibilities of actions to take. Ask yourself:

- What can I do about the situation?
- What might be a first step?
- What might interfere with my taking this step?
- What consequences might I fear, which could block my action?
- How can I handle any consequences or interferences?
- What second or third steps could I take?
- How would these actions take into account everyone involved?
- How would I like to feel when this is over?

Outcomes of Expanding Your Awareness (Prior to Making a Future Action Plan)

As you expand your awareness, often your angry feelings start to change. That is because feelings by themselves function like a barometer indicating your emotional climate. It is very difficult, if not impossible, simply to stop being angry or to change how you feel by only (or continually) focusing just on your angry feeling.

Rather, the best way to handle your feeling of anger is to understand what is going on, and to alter, if necessary, other parts of your Wheel. Since all parts of your Awareness Wheel interconnect and influence each other, significant, positive change in any other part will be reflected in a change in your anger.

Along with your reflection comes an internal quieting (shift in your feeling) as you begin to align the parts of your Wheel and discover your next step. Often a simple integration or *knowing* emerges, which seems right and is congruent rather than fragmented (the more common experience of unhealthy anger).

Answers do not always emerge immediately. Sometimes it takes several periods of reflection plus perhaps talking with your partner or another person, about your alternatives. The main thing is to remain honest with yourself, counting yourself and any others involved. Expanding your awareness will help you do one of two things:

- Confirm your experience and the appropriateness of your anger as a basis for a strong, congruent, next step.

- Reconfigure your experience of the situation (such as get more data, change your thinking and expectations, or alter your wants) to move past your anger to a constructive outcome.

Understanding permits you to release your negative energy in a congruent and healthy way to resolve your disturbance.

STEP 3: MAKE A FUTURE ACTION PLAN

Now you can act on your awareness by making a plan. You determine how you will proceed in order to express your anger in a healthy way that brings all the parts of your Wheel together and shows care for yourself and anyone involved. This is congruence.

This step propels you past simply being aware. As valuable as awareness is, if you stop there without actually doing something constructive about your episode of anger, you risk never moving beyond the experience. You may continue to recycle it.[5]

Several kinds of constructive future actions are possible.

Engage Person in Conversation (If Focus is a Person)

Use the talking and listening skills to connect. Keep the notion of leading and following in mind as you plan to converse. Remember, the other person (your partner, for instance) does not need to use the skills for you to manage yourself effectively and thus positively influence the situation. Do a rehearsal of how you plan to proceed. (Use your skills mat to rehearse, if necessary, or write down a possible sequence.)

Change Your Behavior Toward the Focus

Sometimes it is not possible or you choose not to talk directly to the focus person. In such a case, you can change your behavior toward the other person and alter the way you relate, without telling him or her what you are doing. (The challenge here is to act congruently and not slip into an unhealthy way of relating.) For example:

- Stop contributing to the situation in the way you have done in the past. (For instance, no longer cover for someone else's negative actions for which you may have become over-responsible.)

- Figure some ways to respond differently to the focus.

- Identify ways to connect with the other person (if the focus is a person) without aiming to change him or her. (Sometimes you can direct an inordinate amount of effort in trying to change — attempting to control — the other person, which rarely succeeds. Generally, it creates resistance in that person.)

Determine, as you experiment with the new behavior, to be aware of other parts of your Awareness Wheel, particularly your feelings. You may wish to rehearse the behavior prior to putting it into effect.

Release

Intentionally let the anger go. If the focus of your anger has been towards another person, you need not ever talk about it to the person who was the focus. Decide to move on to other aspects of your life or relationships and not stay stuck with your anger. Choose to set the anger aside.

(Releasing your anger probably cannot happen effectively without the prior step of expanding your awareness fully about it. Letting your anger go does not imply that you have avoided it, but rather having faced and accepted it, you have altered your thinking about its meaning and effect on your life. You have likely modified your wants and actions regarding the focus.)

In releasing the anger, you realize that the longer-term effects upon yourself and anyone else involved are more beneficial by not maintaining it, and these effects outweigh those of continuing it. You may even take the next step, which is to forgive the other person.

Seek Help

If you have difficulty acting congruently immediately, or your Time Out does not produce the outcomes you aim for, you may choose to seek help from an outside, trusted resource. You may go to a pastor, counselor, marriage and family therapist, or some other competent and trusted person who can aid you in sorting through your awareness and setting actions that will be more satisfying.

DEALING WITH AN ANGER HANGOVER

You can expend an enormous amount of energy dealing with anger, particularly when you have expressed your emotion in an unhealthy way. You may have embarrassed yourself and others, or made matters worse by hurting your partner (or someone else) emotionally, as well. Plus the event has typically stimulated and aroused a number of metabolic functions in your body. Often, after such an episode, you feel an emotional and mental drain. This fatigue is an anger hangover.

Sometimes recovery calls for:

- Sleep and some rest.

- A debriefing — post-talk — time to expand your awareness further with your partner or someone else. The purpose is to learn about yourself and determine what you will do differently in the future.

- A sincere apology, even the asking of forgiveness.

USEFULNESS OF ANGER

The emotion of anger can produce some positive outcomes. These include:

Protection

Anger provides healthy boundaries. It builds a wall against the focus of the anger, which helps when the focus could be harmful. Anger can bring action in a dangerous or fearful situation, and the action can serve to bring you to safety.

Emotional Freedom

Anger can break through fear and pain or blocks to other emotions. When you figure out your anger, you may recognize deeper and more central emotions, which you in turn can explore. Once you have done that, you gain freedom to move on in life.

Justice and Human Rights

Anger can motivate and generate actions that help alter society positively against injustices, for broader human rights.

Proaction

Anger may force questions and the seeking of answers for useful change.

GENERALIZATIONS ABOUT ANGER

Several overall generalizations about the emotion of anger include:

- Certain states make a person more vulnerable to anger, such as fatigue, anxiety, pressure or high levels of stress, and illness.

- Relationship difficulty often occurs when partners express the energy in anger differently.

- Others draw back from expressions (even inward ones) of anger. Ways in which this occurs include:

  - Sharing the expression of anger does not bring people closer together in the way that sharing the expression of other feelings (joy, sadness, etcetera) does.

  - Some people express anger at their partner inappropriately in the the presence of others (for example, in front of friends, relatives, or in a public place) and use the others as an audience to vent, displace, or leak anger at their partner. This violates boundaries and often causes others to move away and feel uncomfortable.

  - Involved people get more separate.

- Anger is usually expressed in a place or situation where we feel safe to do so.

- Venting anger, including physical venting, increases rather than reduces aggression.[6]

ADVANTAGES OF MANAGING YOUR ANGER

In addition to understanding the components of anger, applying healthy ways to manage and use anger constructively will help you in several ways. Most likely you will gain more satisfaction in how you relate to your partner and others, a healthier life, and a better sense of well-being. No doubt you will experience an overall increase in the productivity of your efforts, as well.

Finally, knowing that you possess choice about what to do when the feeling of anger arises in you gives you an added measure of freedom in your life.

PARTNER DISCUSSIONS

- Talk about how you saw your parents handle their anger toward one another. How has that influenced the unhealthy or healthy ways you express anger?

- Tell your partner about a positive experience you have had recently managing your own anger. Use Pre-Talk, if you think it would be useful, to tell your partner that you would like him or her simply to share your progress.

MANAGING MY ANGER IN A TIME OUT

Instructions:
1. When you find yourself having recurrent feelings of anger focused on a particular person or situation, follow this strategy to manage your anger effectively.

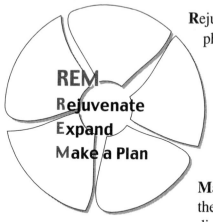

Rejuvenate yourself in a way that will calm your physiology. (See suggestions on pages 93-94.)

Expand your awareness
Use your Awareness Wheel Pad (supplied with your COUPLE COMMUNICATION II Couple Packet) to fill out your awareness about the issue or situation, to help you understand it. (Review pages 94-99.)

Make a future action plan that will be constructive for the situation and for the longer term. (See options discussed on pages 99-101.) Circle the plan on your pad to highlight your commitment.

2. Next, rehearse putting your strategy into practice. If helpful, use your lap mat or the set of large floor mats.

3. Ask yourself, "What have I learned about myself from this situation?"

RESPONDING TO MY PARTNER'S ANGER

Choosing to Escalate or De-Escalate

4

Responding to My Partner's Anger

When your partner is angry, you and your relationship are affected by the anger. If the anger is expressed in your presence, you experience the emotional climate it generates, whether or not the focus of it is toward you or toward an event, object, or other person outside your relationship. Even when your partner expresses the anger away from you, yet brings home its residue or its result, it influences the quality of your time together. While you receive an impact, its form may differ depending on whether the anger is expressed in an unhealthy or a healthy way.

How *you* respond when your partner expresses anger can make a difference in the climate of your relationship. Your response can increase the negativity of your time together, lessen its effect, or help turn the situation into a more positive experience for both of you. While you cannot control your partner's emotion, you can manage your own response, and this contributes to the overall climate. You always have choice in how you relate.

ANGER AND STYLES OF COMMUNICATION

Expressions of anger fall into one of the Styles of Communication, although for someone who holds in his or her anger, the specific style is less clear. The person who holds in anger often falls silent or relies on Small and Shop Talk.

EXPRESSIONS OF ANGER

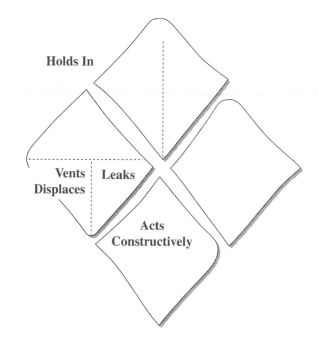

Holds In

Vents
Displaces

Leaks

Acts
Constructively

Your *response* to your partner's anger corresponds with one of the Styles of Communication, too. Consider the various possibilities of response from the chart across the page. As your partner expresses his or her anger in a particular way during an angry episode, you can persist in a certain style yourself or actually switch from one style to another as you respond. The differing options of your response ultimately influence how the overall interaction goes. This becomes particularly important when your partner vents, displaces, leaks, or holds in the anger in an unhealthy way, although it still applies if your partner acts constructively. Whatever the expression, your response style is significant. (For a full discussion of Styles of Communication, review Chapter 4 in *Talking and Listening Together.*[1])

VARIOUS RESPONSE STYLES

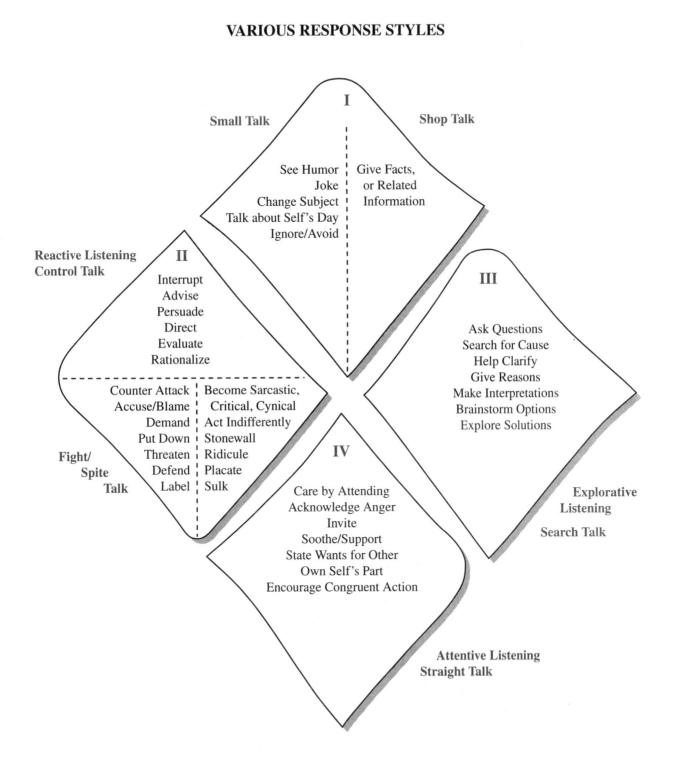

I

Small Talk   Shop Talk

See Humor | Give Facts,
Joke | or Related
Change Subject | Information
Talk about Self's Day |
Ignore/Avoid |

Reactive Listening
Control Talk

II

Interrupt
Advise
Persuade
Direct
Evaluate
Rationalize

Counter Attack | Become Sarcastic,
Accuse/Blame | Critical, Cynical
Demand | Act Indifferently
Put Down | Stonewall
Threaten | Ridicule
Defend | Placate
Label | Sulk

Fight/
Spite
Talk

III

Ask Questions
Search for Cause
Help Clarify
Give Reasons
Make Interpretations
Brainstorm Options
Explore Solutions

Explorative
Listening

Search Talk

IV

Care by Attending
Acknowledge Anger
Invite
Soothe/Support
State Wants for Other
Own Self's Part
Encourage Congruent Action

Attentive Listening
Straight Talk

EXAMPLES OF RESPONSES TO EXPRESSIONS OF ANGER

Since how you respond to anger makes a difference, think about what might be the course of the interaction in the following situations, depending upon the particular response styles used.

Style Responses to Venting

For example: You and your partner have plans to go out to dinner and you arrive later than agreed upon, so your partner becomes angry. Venting in Fight Talk, your partner says to you:

> "You're late again. You're never on time. You always wreck our plans!"

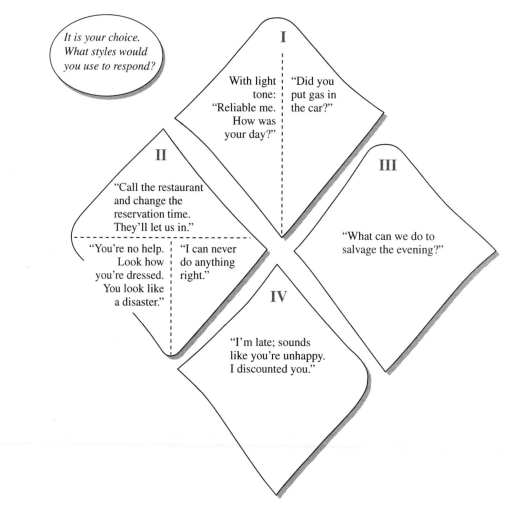

It is your choice. What styles would you use to respond?

I

With light tone: "Reliable me. How was your day?" | "Did you put gas in the car?"

II

"Call the restaurant and change the reservation time. They'll let us in."

"You're no help. Look how you're dressed. You look like a disaster." | "I can never do anything right."

III

"What can we do to salvage the evening?"

IV

"I'm late; sounds like you're unhappy. I discounted you."

Style Responses to Displacing

For example: Your partner is angry about the traffic jam on the way home from work. Displacing the anger upon arrival at home, your partner snarls at you:

"What are you watching that stupid TV show for? Where's some food around here? You're so disorganized!"

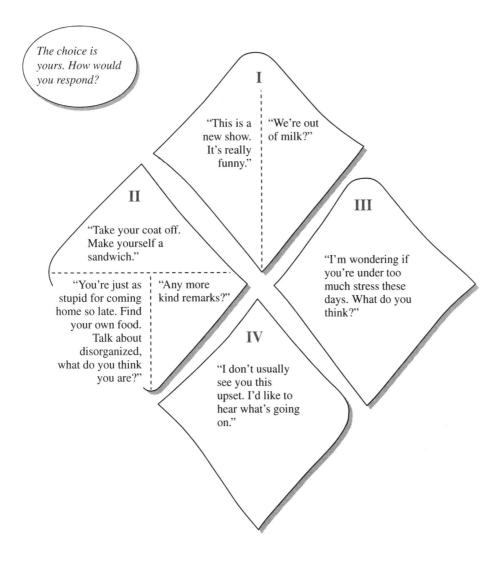

The choice is yours. How would you respond?

I

"This is a new show. It's really funny." | "We're out of milk?"

II

"Take your coat off. Make yourself a sandwich."

"You're just as stupid for coming home so late. Find your own food. Talk about disorganized, what do you think you are?" | "Any more kind remarks?"

III

"I'm wondering if you're under too much stress these days. What do you think?"

IV

"I don't usually see you this upset. I'd like to hear what's going on."

Style Responses to Leaking

During an afternoon picnic sponsored by your company, your partner makes periodic sarcastic remarks about you and the kind of work you do. Then as you drive away, your partner says in a flat tone of voice,

"Well, that was a thrill and a half."

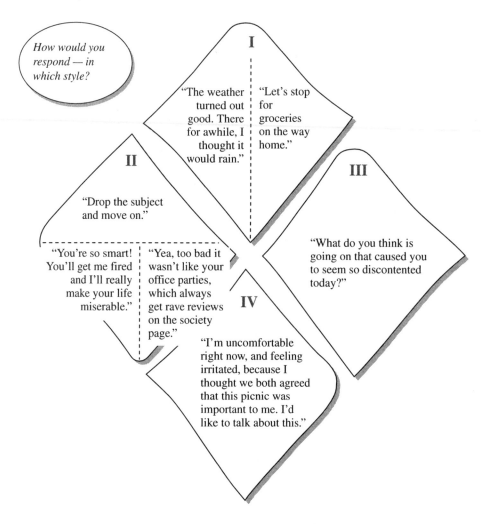

How would you respond — in which style?

I

"The weather turned out good. There for awhile, I thought it would rain."

"Let's stop for groceries on the way home."

II

"Drop the subject and move on."

"You're so smart! You'll get me fired and I'll really make your life miserable."

"Yea, too bad it wasn't like your office parties, which always get rave reviews on the society page."

III

"What do you think is going on that caused you to seem so discontented today?"

IV

"I'm uncomfortable right now, and feeling irritated, because I thought we both agreed that this picnic was important to me. I'd like to talk about this."

Style Responses to Holding In

Your partner is quiet, yet you notice a deep frown on your partner's face.

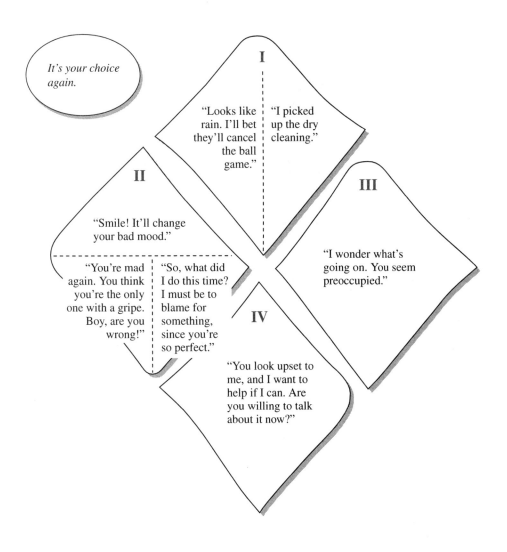

It's your choice again.

I

"Looks like rain. I'll bet they'll cancel the ball game." | "I picked up the dry cleaning."

II

"Smile! It'll change your bad mood."

"You're mad again. You think you're the only one with a gripe. Boy, are you wrong!" | "So, what did I do this time? I must be to blame for something, since you're so perfect."

III

"I wonder what's going on. You seem preoccupied."

IV

"You look upset to me, and I want to help if I can. Are you willing to talk about it now?"

MY TYPICAL RESPONSES TO PARTNER'S ANGER

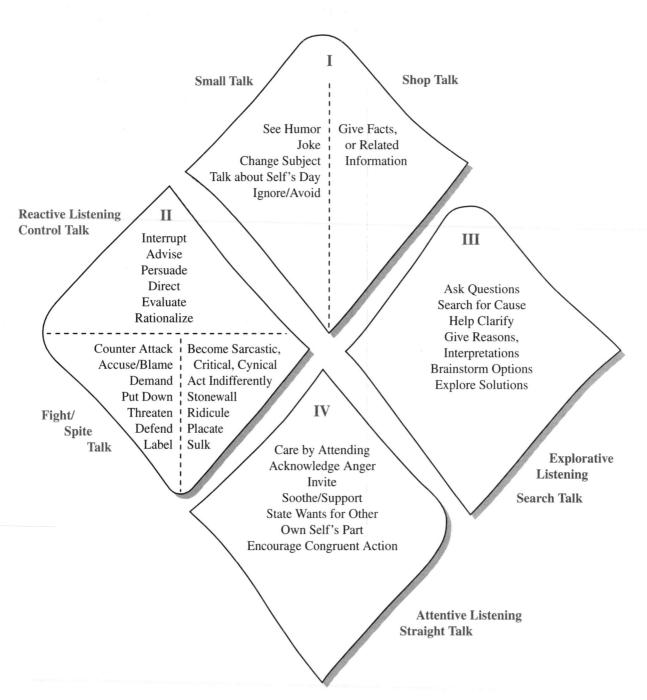

I

Small Talk   **Shop Talk**

See Humor ¦ Give Facts,
Joke ¦ or Related
Change Subject ¦ Information
Talk about Self's Day ¦
Ignore/Avoid ¦

Reactive Listening
Control Talk   **II**

Interrupt
Advise
Persuade
Direct
Evaluate
Rationalize

III

Counter Attack ¦ Become Sarcastic,
Accuse/Blame ¦ Critical, Cynical
Demand ¦ Act Indifferently
Put Down ¦ Stonewall
Threaten ¦ Ridicule
Defend ¦ Placate
Label ¦ Sulk

Ask Questions
Search for Cause
Help Clarify
Give Reasons,
Interpretations
Brainstorm Options
Explore Solutions

Fight/
Spite
Talk

IV

Care by Attending
Acknowledge Anger
Invite
Soothe/Support
State Wants for Other
Own Self's Part
Encourage Congruent Action

Explorative
Listening

Search Talk

Attentive Listening
Straight Talk

Instructions:

1. Circle your partner's typical unhealthy expression of anger:
   Vent   Displace   Leak   Hold In

2. Look across the page to note ways of responding in the various styles.

3. When you hear or see your partner expressing anger in the way you circled, what styles are typical of how you respond to his or her anger? Give approximate percentages of your response styles.

4. Write your typical ways of responding to your partner's expression of anger.

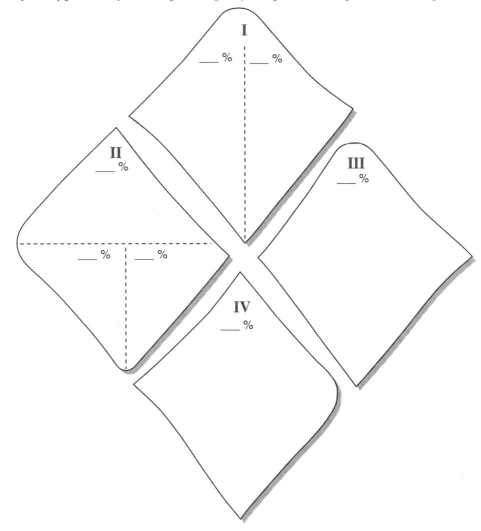

4. Share this with your partner.

RECOGNIZING YOUR OWN AWARENESS

How you respond to your partner's anger depends in large part on your internal experience at the time — your own thoughts, feelings, and wants as you see and hear your partner's distress.

Keep in mind that what goes on inside of you could be entirely different from what your partner experiences in the same situation. Remember that you and your partner possess individual, separate Awareness Wheels. For example, in one instance, what your partner becomes fired off about can seem insignificant or even funny to you. At another time, a catalyst in you ignites in relation to your partner's anger, and you in turn, become angry, though from a different thought, feeling, or want than your partner's.

Realizing the uniqueness of your separate experiences and being clear about your own awareness frees you to respond effectively to your partner's anger. (In addition, knowing what activates the catalysts within you helps you manage the arousal that might also occur in you when your partner is angry.)

For instance, what do you usually *think* about your partner's anger? If you think your partner is immature or inconsiderate for becoming angry in public, your belief will color your response.

What are your own typical *feelings* in response to your partner's anger? Do you feel fear, contempt, disgust, compassion, or concern? Do you in turn often feel angry yourself? For example, if you feel disgust, your reaction could be to give a sarcastic insult back to your partner.

What do you *want* for yourself or your partner during an episode of his or her anger? If, for instance, you are concerned with your own desire to avoid a scene, you will respond in a certain way.

What are your typical *actions?* (These likely include some of your responses for the preceding exercise.)

MY AWARENESS OF MY OWN RESPONSE

Instructions: What goes on in your own experience when your partner expresses his or her anger. What is typical for you?

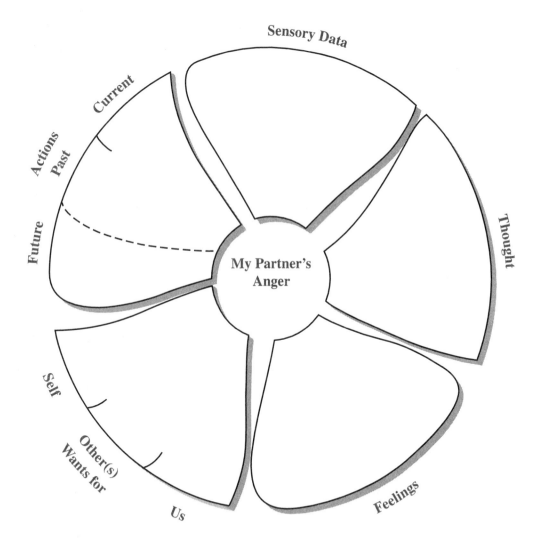

Share this awareness with your partner.

TO ESCALATE OR DE-ESCALATE THE ANGER

When your partner is angry, whether at a focus outside your relationship or at you, your responses serve to do one of three possibilities:

1. Escalate the anger.

2. Maintain the anger (it stays the same).

3. De-escalate the anger.

**TYPICAL RESULTS OF
STYLE CHOICES**

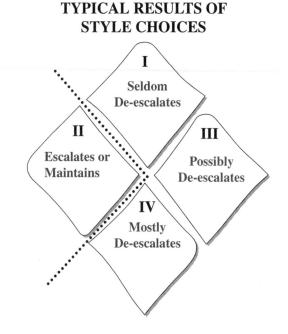

Using a particular style in response to anger can increase the chance of one of the three possibilities occurring.

Consider Style II responses. Control, Fight and Spite Talk or Reactive Listening usually turn up the pressure and amplify the angry emotion, making things worse (escalating the anger). Typical Style II attempts to be helpful that generally escalate the anger, or at least maintain it, include:

"Don't worry about it."

It's no big deal."

"I told you so."

"Forget about it."

"You're crazy to let that upset you."

"Don't feel that way."

"You'll get over it."

> If you think you are in any physical danger from your partner's anger, leave immediately. Go to a safe place.

The other styles (Style I, III, and IV responses) vary in their effectiveness for influencing de-escalation.

Consider Style I. Sometimes a joke about (Small Talk response) or a move away from your partner's anger can be very effective in relieving tension; however, these actions can backfire and serve to throw fuel on the fire. Factual information (Small or Shop Talk) rarely decreases anger successfully. Overall, Style I seldom de-escalates strong emotion.

The headier Style III of Search Talk and Explorative Listening look for causes or solutions in a more rational way. These actions possibly de-escalate, or at least can be steps to begin de-escalation. However, this style by itself often fails to connect with the emotional steam driving the situation.

Style IV aims at connecting directly with the heavy emotion, making it the most likely style to de-escalate the anger. The skills of Attentive Listening and Straight Talk hear the distressing content and provide nurture to the relationship. This style offers the greatest capacity to engage the feelings, dealing with the upsetting situation in the most successful way.

TO CONTROL OR TO CONNECT

When someone is angry, the first response of most people is to protect and defend themselves — their physical body as well as their thoughts, feelings, or wants — by moving away or attempting to control the other's experience of the anger. They try to make the anger go away or prevent it from getting out of hand. To reach these objectives with another's anger, most of us have learned to use Style I or II behaviors. These styles appear to be natural and seemingly efficient as responses. However, the attempt to control another person, particularly in anger, often breeds counter-control responses, and it typically escalates or at least maintains the tension.

INTENTIONS

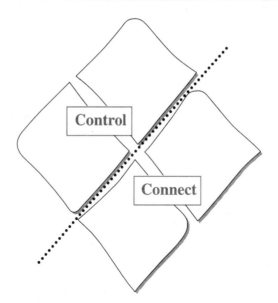

An alternative to the attempt to control is to connect with the person who is angry. This means engaging the other's underlying pain or distress with a caring attitude, and it can be done by applying Style III and particularly Style IV communication in specific ways. Connecting is much more effective in de-escalating anger.

While this type of response works better, usually it does not come naturally and it must be learned. Yet discovering how to connect in such a distressing situation is especially important when the anger is aimed at you. Perhaps the greatest opportunity and challenge for finding skillful, effective ways to connect and engage occur when the strong emotion is directed at you by your partner.

Thus, recognize that in responding to anger, your intention — to control or to connect — is critical. In distressing, angry situations, consider what your intentions are and ask yourself, "Am I trying to protect my own comfort zone and control my partner, or am I trying to connect with and engage my partner's experience?" Honesty with yourself about your own motive makes a big difference in the way you respond.

Your Interaction Choices

While you cannot control your partner's angry expression, you are able to influence his or her anger by managing yourself and choosing how you respond.

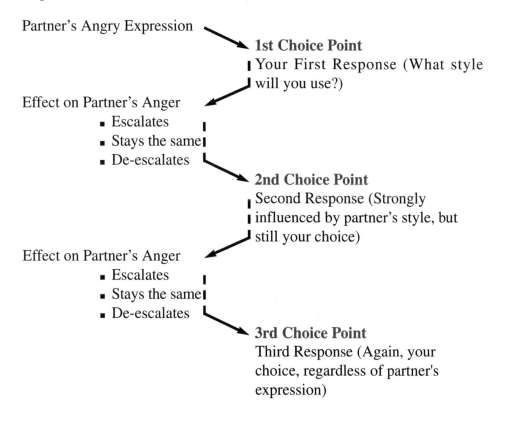

Partner's Angry Expression

1st Choice Point
Your First Response (What style will you use?)

Effect on Partner's Anger
- Escalates
- Stays the same
- De-escalates

2nd Choice Point
Second Response (Strongly influenced by partner's style, but still your choice)

Effect on Partner's Anger
- Escalates
- Stays the same
- De-escalates

3rd Choice Point
Third Response (Again, your choice, regardless of partner's expression)

When Your First Attempt Fails

Suppose your angry partner vents, displaces, or leaks in Fight or Spite Talk, and your first response — in Small Talk humor or with an Explorative Listening question — is not effective. Your partner continues to use Fight or Spite Talk. The natural tendency is to join him or her in Fight or Spite Talk and extend the negative exchange.

Importance of Your Second Response

You can resist joining your partner's negative style. If your first response does not achieve the de-escalation, you still have choice at your second response. For example, use of Style-IV skills to reflect your partner's awareness by giving an "acknowledgement" or "want for other" repeats the attempt to connect.

Your Choices Continue

Even at your third response, you continue to have choice in how you relate. In fact, your responses all along the way are something you decide, regardless of what your partner does. Once you realize this, you can experiment with style options that you believe will be helpful for the situation.

Reflecting on Your Choices of Response

It is useful to consider what your response choices have been, at several points, when your partner has been angry. Think about the styles you have used at your first, second, or third responses. Reflect on whether your words and nonverbals have tended to escalate, maintain, or de-escalate the emotion. Also consider whether a change of style that you might have employed along the way has created a positive turning point in the anger.

What you do at each of the choice points makes a difference in the ultimate course of the interaction. Thus, while you cannot control your partner and his or her angry emotion, you hold power to affect and influence how that anger continues to be expressed.

MY INTERACTIVE RESPONSES TO MY PARTNER'S ANGER

Instructions: Recall a situation in which your partner expressed his or her anger. Now think about the sequence of your responses to this anger. (Give examples of words and other behaviors.)

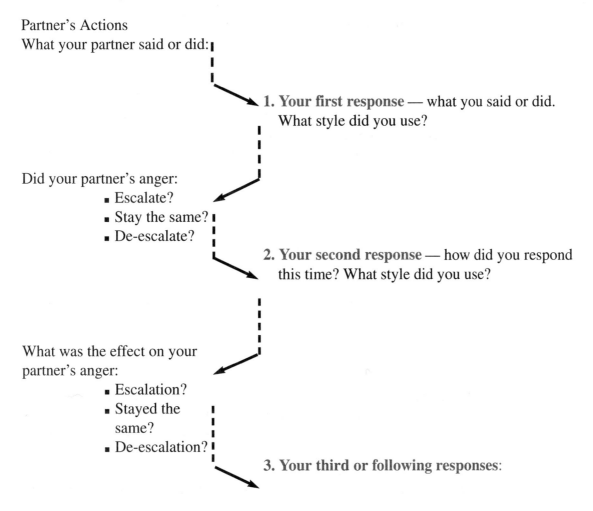

Partner's Actions
What your partner said or did:

1. Your first response — what you said or did. What style did you use?

Did your partner's anger:
- Escalate?
- Stay the same?
- De-escalate?

2. Your second response — how did you respond this time? What style did you use?

What was the effect on your partner's anger:
- Escalation?
- Stayed the same?
- De-escalation?

3. Your third or following responses:

4. Did you create a positive turning point?

5. Share this with your partner.

RESPONDING BY CONNECTING

When you desire to respond to your partner's anger by connecting with him or her and the distress, you apply particular actions and skills. These help you manage yourself to influence the situation positively.

PREREQUISITE: CARING

Caring about your partner, as well as yourself, is a prerequisite to connecting effectively. Without a caring attitude, your actions, even though skilled, will come across as manipulative and be experienced as an attempt to control.

REU

The actions and skills for connecting translate into three major steps. To help you remember more easily, think of them as the REU steps.

R E U
Recognize and Rebalance
Engage Partner's Anger
Understand Partner's Situation More Fully

STEP 1. RECOGNIZE AND REBALANCE

This two-part step means to recognize nonverbal and verbal cues in your partner and to rebalance yourself physically.

Recognize Cues in Your Partner

Nonverbal Cues

Your partner, as everyone else, possesses a unique *body signature* — pattern of nonverbal behaviors that occur in a variety of situations. Part of the nonverbal body signature is the expression of anger, which signals distress. One aspect of getting to know your partner involves learning to recognize his or her nonverbal cues that show the emotion of anger (as well as the cues for other emotions, too).

The nonverbal cues precede and are probably more powerful than any words that are spoken. Nonverbal cues for anger include:

- Facial expressions (tightness, flushed, or possibly ashen if holding in)

- Labored breathing

- Gestures (more expansive and linear, or if holding in, more constrained)

- Body tension and posture (upper body more rigid with venting and displacing)

- Accentuated actions (harsher, louder, and more forceful with venting and displacing or more obtuse, reserved and tentative with leaking and holding in)

- Possible tears

- Tone of voice (ranging, for example, from harsh, loud, whiney, brittle, shrill, or strident to monosyllabic or tired-sounding)

Word Cues

Verbal cues come from words in the communication styles of Fight Talk, Spite Talk, or even Control Talk that has an edge to the tone used. For example, words such as, " You always," tied to an accusation often signal anger. The question of "Why" that challenges or blames shows anger, too. These styles typically display an uncaring attitude. Sometimes, depending on the person, no talk at all signals anger, when it would be usual for the person to converse.

Recognizing the specific nonverbal and verbal cues your partner displays will help you, early on, respond more effectively to the anger. Sometimes you can recognize the cues very quickly.

Rebalance Yourself

When you see tension in your partner and his or her specific expression of anger, the natural tendency is to follow suit and tighten up yourself. (For example, it is particularly hard to listen when you think your partner is criticizing you. The typical urge is to defend yourself and try to correct your partner's thinking, which is really an attempt to control. This creates tension in you, too.) So at this point, it is very important to manage your own anxiety and the arousal of stress that may occur in you. Usually it takes being intentional about your actions.

Take a Breath and Attend

At the point of recognizing your partner's tension, take a quiet, deep breath and let the muscles throughout your body relax. Attend (look and listen) to your partner. Sometimes you may also find it useful to suggest, "Let's both take a relaxing breath."

EXERCISE: MY PARTNER'S ANGER CUES

1. Think about the cues that your partner gives which let you know he or she is angry. What are his or her specific signals?

   Nonverbal (body) cues:

   > Facial expression
   >
   > Breathing
   >
   > Gestures
   >
   > Body tension/posture
   >
   > Actions
   >
   > Tone of voice, pitch, and pace

   Verbal cues:

   > Actual words

2. What are typical ways that you react negatively to these cues?

3. How can you make use of these cues to help your partner?

4. Discuss the cues with your partner.

Change State Physically

As part of rebalancing yourself, consider changing your physical state and suggest this to your partner, too. For example,

- If you are sitting, stand up.
- Go for a walk.
- Change context, such as move to a different room.
- Offer a drink of water.

If you can both move physically, it will alter your own, as well as your partner's breathing. Generally such a change helps slow down the interaction, and it has a calming effect on your angry partner, making him or her more receptive to the next step.

Taking a breath, attending, and changing state help you avoid getting caught up in your partner's tension and indicate your receptivity to connecting with his or her distress.

Rebalancing has a softening effect on your body that supports successful anger management and conflict resolution. As your face relaxes, you show calmness (rather than tension). When you talk, your voice will be lower (and not so reactive). Your partner will in turn generally relax as he or she sees you managing yourself rather than escalating the anger in the situation.

STEP 2. ENGAGE MY PARTNER'S ANGER

Engaging means to demonstrate care for your partner by connecting with the angry emotion he or she is experiencing. To do this effectively implies that you set aside or transcend your own immediate interests in order to show love and care to your partner.

As long as the adrenaline is rising, and the physiology overtakes the rationality, you cannot try to help your partner think through the situation in any logical way. Rather, you must relate first to your partner's emotion, focusing on process instead of the content or outcome. This will help you de-escalate the anger.

Draw on Specific Skills To Engage

Recall that in Chapter 2, the talking and listening skills are further designated as *leading* or *following* behaviors. The leading refers to the six talking skills plus the skill called Ask Open Questions. The following refers to the other listening skills.

While all eleven communication skills of Attentive Listening, Straight Talk, Explorative Listening and Search Talk are essential, certain ones stand out in responding to anger. As a general rule, particular *following* skills and certain *leading* skills help you to connect with an angry person. If you use these skills with your partner in a caring way, you will often de-escalate the anger.

Following Skills

The following skills of attending, acknowledging, inviting, and summarizing encourage your partner to talk about the distress in a way that goes beyond discharging the emotion. These four listening skills will affirm your partner. More than that, they help you to listen for deeper feelings (fear, hurt, desperation, or sadness), thoughts (meanings), and

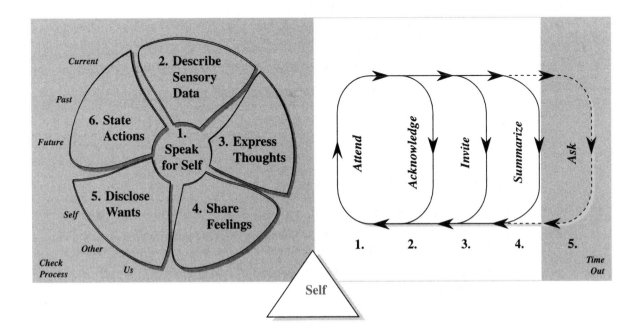

wants (desires) of your partner. Of course, these particular skills allow him or her to release the negative energy, too.

Leading Skills

The leading skills at the far left side of the Awareness Wheel (past, current, and future actions plus wants for other) can be powerful connectors. The action skills help you take responsibility clearly, in a non-defensive way, for your contribution to the situation (if in fact you have contributed). Expressing true wants for your partner (based on the other's real interests) also can be relieving. Your partner realizes that you have his or her interests at heart.

Be aware that if you try to give an interpretation or express your own feelings (even using skills), you will likely find it to backfire on you. (It may escalate things.) This occurs because, at that moment, your partner is probably so aroused and pre-occupied with his or her own troubles, that he or she is unable to show interest or be responsive to your concerns. You must draw upon your own ability to manage yourself, as well as care for your partner.

As you use the skills, try to stay on your skills mat, literally or symbolically.

Beyond Skills

Sometimes a gentle touch (to give support) to your partner in his or her anger shows caring and compassion.

Look for Turning Points

Turning points are moments that show a reversal of the escalation. Typically the de-escalation begins from the use of one or two skills. It can also occur with a modification in your intentions, which you display by a shift in the Style of Communication that you are using. Making small changes can yield big results.

Try to create positive turning points. Watch for them in your partner's nonverbal responses.

When you do something that reduces your partner's tension, you will see and hear it first in his or her body language — the nonverbal communication. As your partner's anger begins to de-escalate, you can observe the:

- Facial expression (softening in face or color less flushed)

- Breathing (more even and calm)

- Body (more relaxed)

- Actions (calmer)

- Tone of voice (quieter, less tension in it)

Your partner's nonverbals reflect your influence — whether or not your actions:

- De-escalate the anger

- Continue or maintain the anger

- Escalate the anger

Anger must be discharged constructively before you can go on to the next step of understanding your partner's situation more fully.

STEP 3. UNDERSTAND MY PARTNER'S SITUATION MORE FULLY

To understand your partner's situation more fully, continue to use the skills to lead and follow as necessary. During this step, apply any or all of the skills in any order as your partner and you understand his or her broader and deeper awareness about what has stimulated the anger and about some of the implications of it.

Remember that pursuing understanding does not necessarily mean that you agree with what your partner is saying. Understanding and agreement are separate activities.

After pursuing and demonstrating accurate understanding, you could help your partner put the anger to work constructively. With your aid, he or she might want to take action by generating a solution.

Keep in mind, however, that sometimes understanding itself is the solution. No further action is necessary.

During Any Step

Recall the options of Check Process and Time Out. These options can help you make sure you are dealing with the anger in a way that is working and that you are doing so at an appropriate time and place.

OTHER SUGGESTIONS FOR RESPONDING TO UNHEALTHY EXPRESSIONS OF ANGER

If your partner expresses anger predominantly by venting, displacing, leaking, or holding in, you may find it useful to consider specific suggestions to act responsibly in order to de-escalate the anger. For the particular expression, it is helpful to determine an immediate goal and to find a way to meet it. The next section provides options and examples of specific ways to respond to the various unhealthy expressions of anger.

VENTING

Immediate Goal: To help your partner de-escalate his or her anger.

Example Situation: Your partner is upset with you for not having recorded a check that led to an overdraft at your bank.

Some examples of leading and following responses to reach the goal appear below. (Leading responses are shaded, while the following responses are not.) The dots indicate the skills most likely to engage your partner.

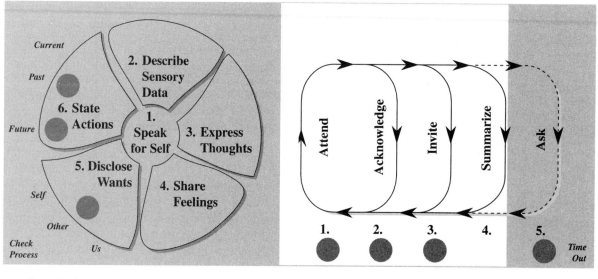

Past Action
"I didn't record the check as I should have."
Wants for Other
"I'd like for you to feel confident about what is in our checking account."
Future Action
"I'll make sure that I record checks after this."

Attend
Look and listen.
Acknowledge
"Irritating."
"No follow-though."
"Annoying."
Action/Invite
"This is hard for me to hear, but keep talking." *(Combines brief comment with listening to care for self and respond to other.)*

Ask
"How much was the overdraft?" *(data)*
"What can we do now?" *(action)*

GENERAL SUGGESTIONS FOR RESPONDING TO VENTING

Once you recognize the anger, which is probably very easy to do, take these actions:

- Rebalance yourself. (Protect yourself physically, if necessary, by leaving the area.)

- Acknowledge the feelings, the thoughts, or any wants your partner discloses or that you infer.

- Continue to acknowledge.

- State any actions you have done to help contribute to the anger, if the anger is towards you.

- Tell your partner your wants for him or her in the situation.

- Ask open questions of any parts left unclear, such as, "What do you want?" or "What do you think?"

- State any future action you will do to help the situation.

- Consider combining a talking skill and a listening skill, such as stating an action and inviting, as a way to care for yourself and for your partner.

DISPLACING

Immediate Goal: To help your partner link his or her anger with the real focus and to de-escalate the emotion.

Example Situation: Your partner comes home lashing out, and you are not sure why.

Some examples of skillful leading and following responses to reach the goal appear below. (The leading responses are shaded, while the following responses are not.) The dots indicate the skills most likely to connect.

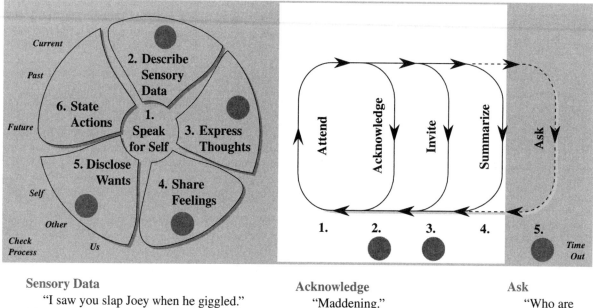

Sensory Data
    "I saw you slap Joey when he giggled."
Thoughts
    "I think something upset you at work."
    "I don't think you're directing your anger at the right person."
Feelings
    "I feel scared when you get into blaming everyone."
Wants for Other
    "I like for you to have a nice evening."

Acknowledge
    "Maddening."
    "Lots of pressure."
    "Too much to do."
    "No recognition."
Invite
    "What's going on?"
    "Say more."

Ask
    "Who are you angry with? *(data)*
    "Do you think you are angry with your job?" *(thought)*

GENERAL SUGGESTIONS FOR RESPONDING TO DISPLACING

The first part is the same as for venting, so once you recognize the anger, take these actions:

- Rebalance yourself. (Protect yourself physically, if necessary, by leaving the area.)

- Acknowledge the feeling (perhaps several times).

- Ask open questions (to discover the real focus of the anger).

- Be sure to keep inviting your partner to talk. (As he or she continues to talk and becomes more emotionally calm with your acknowledgements, he or she can often make a link to the real focus.)

- Tell your partner your wants for him or her in the situation.

- Give (in a gentle way) your own data and thoughts about what might be going on, if you believe it will be helpful.

- Share your own feelings (such as fear or sadness) other than anger (which typically escalates the emotion), if you think it will engage your partner.

LEAKING

Immediate Goal: To help your partner recognize and deal with the anger in the message (or action).

Example Situation: Your partner makes a sarcastic, biting remark to you about the way you look.

Some examples of leading and following responses to reach the goal appear below. (The leading responses are shaded, while the following responses are not.) The dots indicate the skills most likely to result in connecting.

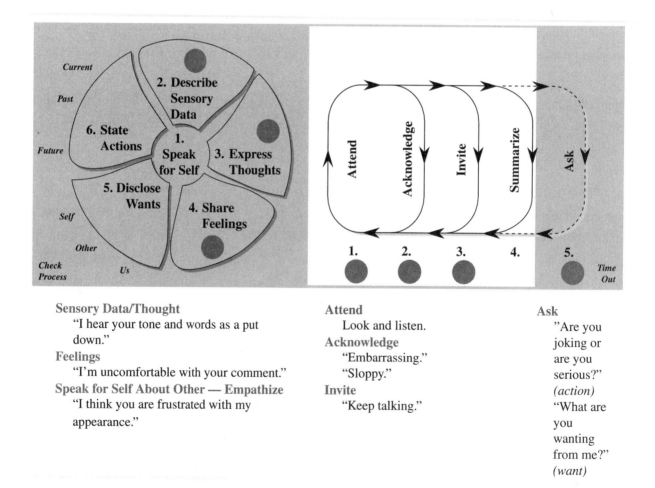

Sensory Data/Thought
   "I hear your tone and words as a put down."
Feelings
   "I'm uncomfortable with your comment."
Speak for Self About Other — Empathize
   "I think you are frustrated with my appearance."

Attend
   Look and listen.
Acknowledge
   "Embarrassing."
   "Sloppy."
Invite
   "Keep talking."

Ask
   "Are you joking or are you serious?"
   (action)
   "What are you wanting from me?"
   (want)

GENERAL SUGGESTIONS FOR RESPONDING TO LEAKING

When you recognize the leaking anger (see or hear spite), take these actions:

- Rebalance yourself.

- Comment on the anger you hear and try to link it with what your partner is experiencing behind the comment or behavior. (This is giving sensory data and your thought.)

- Empathize with your partner's underlying feelings (hurt, anger, disappointment, or sadness) as you attempt to understand his or her Wheel. For example, say, "My guess is you are feeling. . . and thinking. . . and wanting. . ."(Search Talk). The purpose here is to connect with your partner and not to control his or her experience of the situation.

- If you are the focus of the anger, tell how the leaking actions have impacted you (share your feelings), and if you know, how they have affected others involved.

HOLDING IN

Immediate Goal: To draw your partner out and unlock his or her negative energy.

Example Situation: Your partner comes home, does not say hello, and watches TV for a long time without eating supper.

Examples of leading and following responses to reach the goal appear below. The dots indicate the skills most likely to engage your partner.

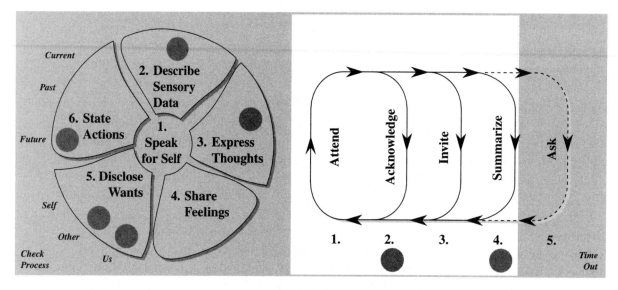

Sensory Data
"I notice you're extra quiet. You didn't say hello and you haven't eaten a thing."

Thoughts
"You seem upset to me."
"I think you must feel hurt or angry about something."

Wants for Other
"I'd like for you to feel contented and not worry."

Want for Us
"I want us to enjoy the evening together."

Future Action:
"I'll listen if you want to talk."

Acknowledge
"Don't feel like talking."
"Hard day."

Summarize
When you partner talks, be sure to demonstrate your understanding by summarizing.

Ask
Asking questions (such as "What's wrong?" or "What do you want?") typically does not work. The other can simply say, "Nothing" and keep holding in.

GENERAL SUGGESTIONS FOR RESPONDING TO HOLDING IN

If your partner holds in his or her anger, you will need to recognize the nonverbal body cues and not depend on your partner's words to disclose the anger.

- Comment on your partner's nonverbals (give sensory data) and express your interpretation of them (thoughts).

- Try to express your partner's Wheel accurately, if you have any idea of what may be bothering him or her. *Speak for self about your partner* — what you think he or she is experiencing. When someone does not talk, talking accurately about what that person is experiencing often engages him or her, either (1) by being empathetically accurate, understanding the situation, or (2) by being off base, necessitating the silent person to speak for himself or herself in order to correct your misunderstanding.

- Perhaps do something that involves your partner in changing his or her physical state. Moving physically changes a person's breathing and can help engage and mobilize negative energy. (If you are sitting, suggest that you stand up together and go for a walk or change context, and move to a different room.) However, pay attention to the context. Your partner will probably feel more comfortable talking about the situation in a private place, without others around.

- Give wants for your partner and relationship.

- Do not push your partner to talk, if he or she is reluctant to do so. Simply ask him or her to consider or reflect on what you have said *(speaking for self about your partner),* and let you know later what he or she thinks about it. Tell him or her you are willing to listen. Then drop matter for the moment. (Consider this as a Time Out.) Continuing to push will only be counterproductive. Do not get trapped in asking many questions with no productive reply to you.

What Works to De-escalate Your Partner's Anger?

The preceding suggestions work in many situations to de-escalate anger, however, to help your particular partner, certain actions may be more useful than others. Plus, additional actions not mentioned here may help in some cases. To discover what these are, recall anything you have done in the past that has served to decrease your partner's anger. Also, discuss with your partner any actions that he or she thinks have worked or would work in the future to bring de-escalation.

WHAT DE-ESCALATES MY PARTNER'S ANGER

Instructions: Talk with your partner about how he or she expresses his or her anger, and how you respond to that. For this exercise, both you and your partner use the small skills mat.

1. What have you done in the past that has de-escalated your partner's anger? Where does that fit with the skills on the mat?

2. What turning points, if any, have you ever noticed?

3. What does your partner want you to do in future situations, which would help create turning points and de-escalate his or her anger ?

MY STRATEGY (ACTION PLAN) FOR RESPONDING TO MY PARTNER'S ANGER

Instructions: Imagine a situation in which your partner might become angry. (You may wish to use the situation you noted on the earlier worksheet, page 115. Or you may choose a new situation, instead.) Determine if the focus of your partner's anger would be at you or at an outside focus.

Below, list skills and actions you can take to help de-escalate the anger and understand the situation more fully. Use any of the suggestions listed earlier for responding to your partner's typical expression of anger. Also use suggestions generated by your discussion with your partner in the preceding exercise.

REU
Recognize and Rebalance
Engage Partner's Anger
Understand Partner's Situation More Fully

Steps (REU) to Help De-Escalate:

Situation:

    R — Recognize and Rebalance

    E — Engage My Partner's Anger

    U — Understand My Partner's Situation More Fully

GENERAL TIPS FOR RESPONDING TO ANGER EFFECTIVELY

- If caught in a negative exchange, stop and shift your behavior. Reach for the skills. Create turning points.

- Ask yourself, "What's my intent — to connect or to control?"

- Ask yourself, "How is my comfort zone being challenged?"

- Do not discount your partner in return when he or she discounts you and shows uncaring behavior to you.

- Do something that relaxes your partner, rather than telling him or her to "Relax!" which usually only increases angry arousal.

- Ask yourself, "What did I learn about responding to anger and managing myself from this situation?"

For the long-term success of your relationship, limiting negative interactions is crucial. Remember that regardless of the way your partner expresses anger, you possess choice about how you behave in response. You can use styles and take actions that increase the negativity of the climate when you are together or that influence it to be more positive.

PARTNER DISCUSSIONS

Stand in Your Partner's Shoes

Instructions: As a way of understanding your partner's anger about a specific situation, fill out a sheet on your Awareness Wheel pad from his or her perspective (imagine being your partner). After you have tried to experience your partner's situation as fully and accurately as possible, show this to him or her and compare your understanding with his or her experience. Talk about what you have discovered and the parts about which you are not sure.

Mutual Anger

The next time you and your partner feel mutually angry with one another, call Time Out and do the following:

1. Each of you use a sheet from your Awareness Wheel pads and fill out an Awareness Wheel on what you think your partner is experiencing. Be careful not to impose what you want him or her to be experiencing.

2. Set a time and place to show one another what you have written and check out what each of you believes the other is experiencing. Do this at a time then you can talk and listen collaboratively.

Re-Connecting

With your partner, discuss the questions below:

1. What do you yourself do that helps you reconnect positively with your partner after a negative exchange?

2. What does your partner do that helps you both reconnect positively after a negative exchange?

Consultant to Third-Party Anger

When your partner is angry with some other person, thing, or event, ask him or her if you could:

1. Be a listener to him or her.

2. Help him or her think through the situation, but not advise about it.

PHASES OF RELATIONSHIP

Aligning Our Dance
Values • Wants • Actions

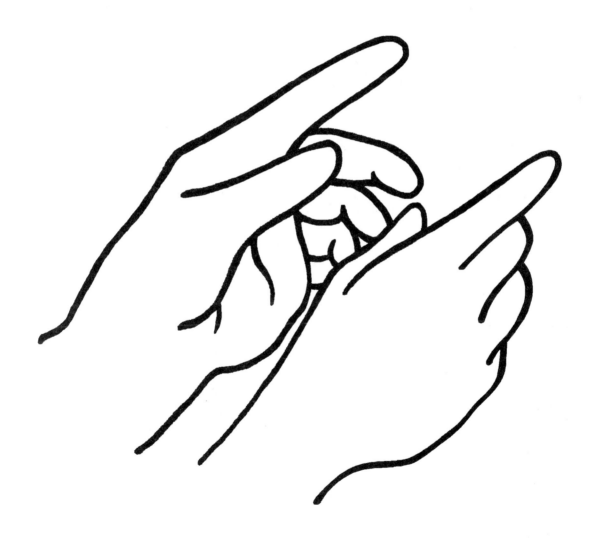

5

Relationship Phases

Over time, the relationship between you and your partner goes through transitions. As life unfolds — revealing what is important to you and the issues that arise at the time — you and your partner alter how you connect with one another. Seldom does a relationship ever stay the same; because life changes, you and your partner modify the ways you relate, too. If you have been together for any length of time, you probably recognize this reality.

With awareness and development of communication skills and processes, plus holding a caring attitude, you can be proactive about how you will relate now and in the future as situations change. You have greater choice, can set goals for yourself and for you as a couple, and determine actions to begin to achieve them.

The changes that you experience over time together can be thought of as happening in phases, periods in which recurrent ways of relating characterize your life together.[1] To reflect on how these various phases fit you and your partner, first answer the questionnaire on the next page, and then read the descriptions that follow.

PHASES OF RELATIONSHIP QUESTIONNAIRE

Instructions: Think about your relationship with you partner as you respond to the following statements. For each item, circle the number on the scale from "never" to "frequently," which best represents your experience of the relationship.

My Partner and I:	Never				Frequently	
1. Talk and dream about our future.	0	1	2	3	4	5
2. Bicker and argue.	0	1	2	3	4	5
3. Go about our own interests and don't bother each other.	0	1	2	3	4	5
4. Stand together as a strong force	0	1	2	3	4	5
5. Figure the things that bother us about one another will probably change in the future.	0	1	2	3	4	5
6. Are in conflict.	0	1	2	3	4	5
7. Try not to rock the boat with each other (to avoid conflict).	0	1	2	3	4	5
8. Work through our disagreements quickly, taking both of us into account.	0	1	2	3	4	5
9. Feel euphoric about each other	0	1	2	3	4	5
10. Tend to blame each other when things don't go right.	0	1	2	3	4	5
11. Talk to someone else — rather than to each other — about things important to each of us.	0	1	2	3	4	5
12. Disclose our vulnerabilities and successes to each other, knowing we can trust one another with the information.	0	1	2	3	4	5
13. Find ourselves anticipating who we will be and things we will do together.	0	1	2	3	4	5
14. Try to change each other.	0	1	2	3	4	5

	Never				**Frequently**	
15. Think other parts of life are more important (to each of us), rather than our relationship, right now.	0	1	2	3	4	5
16. Blend together as a team, using our differences as resources.	0	1	2	3	4	5

So that the scoring of this questionnaire will be more understandable, before you score it, read the descriptions of the four phases that follow.

(A scoring sheet is provided on page 170.)

FOUR PHASES

Four distinctly different phases typically occur during the course of a relationship:

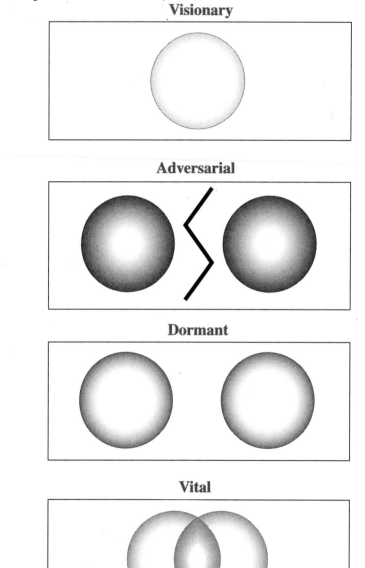

Visionary

Adversarial

Dormant

Vital

As you and your partner experience each one of these phases, you typically feel an increase or a diminishment of satisfaction with one another. Aside from your feelings, each phase brings positive and negative elements.

For many relationships, the movement from one phase to the next occurs in a general progression. For others, a rotation occurs among the phases, which means that once you have been in a phase and moved on to another, you can also return to that previously experienced phase.

You can spend a long time in a particular phase, finding contentment there. Some couples get stuck in a particular phase, and then without moving to the next one, end their relationship, or they continue it with feelings of dissatisfaction and perhaps a pervading negative climate.

If you and your partner possess the ability — the awareness and skills, you can emphasize the positive elements of a phase, reduce the negative ones, or take actions that help you move out of one phase and into another. You can determine what is important for you both now and as you anticipate the future, and make choices that help you to be in alignment with one another — to thrive together as a couple.

VISIONARY PHASE

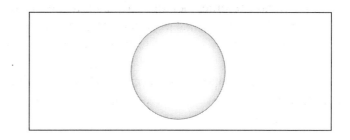

Characteristics of the Visionary Phase

Most couples experience a visionary phase at the beginning of their relationship. However, the visionary phase can occur also at times other than the early part of the relationship. It may happen at important turning points, such as when the last child leaves home or when you anticipate a major move.

During this phase, as the word "visionary" suggests, you both possess an imagined view — a vision — of how your relationship will be. You picture a satisfying future together. You emphasize the value of your similarities and enjoy the way they bond you together. You find your differences stimulating and energy-producing.

You see what you want to see in one another. Each of you also sees what you think the other person envisions in your relationship, and you are attracted to what you see. You believe, that with one another, you can make whatever you want to happen, and barring that, it would not matter, as long as you are together.

While in this visionary phase, you experience a heightened level of excitement. Your feelings are light-hearted, sometimes even to the point of being euphoric. More playfulness goes on, and it feels good. You delight in the fact that you make a difference to someone, that you have a common purpose, and that you share something special.

In terms of the Relationship Map, in this phase, when you are together, your time is mainly positive togetherness. When you are apart, you long for the time to be together again, both believing it will be good.

Often you believe that you have found the one — the answer to life. This answer revolves around the other person and lies outside of yourself. You do what you can to please the other person — to keep that person happy, even if it does not take your own longer-term contentment into account.

You are actually *dependent* upon one another to give meaning to life, to provide esteem, and to supply a purpose; for without the other person, each of you would be lost.

The Focus

In the visionary phase, you focus on:
   us and our immediate future as a couple

You look at what you will do — and at what you will be together. You pay attention to the good features of your relationship, even if that involves ignoring other parts of reality.

Positives and Negatives

The visionary phase definitely provides a positive impact on a relationship. If it is at the beginning of your relationship, it gets you off to a good start. In this phase you set a direction and often make or fantasize your goals. You find motivation to make changes, and you experience optimism about life. You sense your possibilities.

Yet, while you have heightened vision, you may also possess "blurred" vision. When you see what you want to see, you may miss other parts of what is there, especially anything negative about one another or the picture you want to create. (This explains why many couples, when in this phase, avoid programs that are designed to equip them for their relationship long-term, believing for themselves it would not be relevant.)

Also negatively, during this phase, it is easy to deny aspects of the relationship that do not fit right. You discount or ignore parts of yourself or of your partner that interfere with the vision coming to pass. You think that just by virtue of your being together, the negatives will change or go away. To protect the vision, you may unintentionally live with a measure of personal dishonesty. If you do find something that brings doubt, you deny its importance or say to yourself, "That will change later."

Furthermore, in this phase a pressure can begin to build to live up to the expectations that your partner holds for you or that you hold for yourself. For example, "My new job requires extra long hours. Making decisions and doing the upkeep involved in owning our own house seems like it could be more of a demanding chore than a step on the way to our dream. As a result, I procrastinate on activities involved with the house. However I won't admit that this is so for fear of ruining our dream — and perhaps our relationship."

Even with the negative aspects, however, the visionary phase can be a heady, wonderful period in the course of a relationship. The relationship holds high priority for both partners. You hope; you dream. You believe you can overcome any obstacles.

OUR VISIONARY PHASE

Instructions: Think back over your relationship with your partner, perhaps to the beginning of it. Reflect on the visions you shared with one another, and then answer the questions below.

   1. How did you see one another?

         What were your visions about your partner?

         What visions do you think your partner had about you?

   2. What were your visions about the two of you together?

   3. What goals or dreams, if any, did you talk about together?

   4. What aspect of your relationship did you ignore or discount that might have interfered with the visions coming to pass?

Tell your partner about the visions, as you saw them.

ADVERSARIAL PHASE

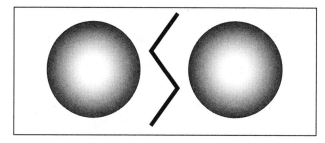

Characteristics of the Adversarial Phase

After awhile partners find that the vision is dimmer than anticipated. Things are not just the way you thought they would be. Reality sets in. As the daily activities and challenges overshadow the initial glow, it is easy to feel frustration, disappointment, or disillusionment that life or your partner is not what you expected it (or him or her) to be. Issues arise that cannot be put on hold, and they bring struggles about how to handle them.

Now, instead of denying the incongruent parts of your relationship or other realities, as you did in the visionary phase, you see them clearly. Perhaps, you even see the aspects that do not fit as larger than life. Your differences come to the foreground while your similarities recede into the background. Your differences begin to clash, and you really feel their impact. Instead of intriguing you, the differences annoy. It is easy to blame your partner for not living up to the expectation.

You try to influence and change one another to stay or become the way you expected or to treat you as you anticipated. At the same time, you each attempt to maintain your own way of being and of doing things. You make interpretations about the other, leading to statements such as, "If you love me, you would do it like this . . ." Or, "You don't appreciate me for who I am."

In this phase, you and your partner grapple with questions of control, whether or not you ever discuss them directly:

- Who, if either of us, has to change?

- Who gets to decide what?

- How are decisions made?

- What happens when a decision is made that is not mutual?

- How is power distributed between the two of us?

As you work these questions out, you experience more conflicts, either about issues or ways of being or doing. Your conflict patterns take form, and your expressions of anger show themselves.

Considering how The Relationship Map applies, you spend much time initiating and responding to change. Your caring or uncaring attitudes and level of skill determine whether these change activities fall into the positive or the negative climate. Some couples get caught in these negative dances.

In the adversarial phase, you and your partner become counter-dependent. You show what you will stand for, what type of structure you will live with, how you operate, and where the limits are. Your partner does the same, and you test these things in one another. As conflicts arise, resistance runs high. You each still want to be accepted and considered to have worth as you show who you are.

The Focus

In the adversarial phase, the focus is on:
changing you (versus changing me)

In other words, "I focus on you — to change. You focus on me — to change." The idea is that while your partner should change, he or she should let you be are you are, and vice versa.

Positives and Negatives

On the positive side, each of you finds the means to show who you really are. At the same time, like it or not, you are forced to recognize your partner's separate wants, intentions, and modes of operating. You see more sides of one another. While these may not be as you envisioned previously, as they become apparent, you figure out how you will deal with them or work out ways of operating together.

If you apply communication skills for gaining awareness and for negotiating about issues, you can come to know and appreciate one another better. Energy and even a deeper understanding of each other can emerge out of a conflict that may occur. Depending on the level of communication skills applied and your caring or uncaring attitudes, your relationship can become more intimate (as you share more of another side of yourself) or you move apart. You begin acting in ways that take you in either of these directions.

On the negative side, during this phase, a contradictory spirit may grow in your relationship. When that happens, you may start talking as though you believe in the win/lose approach to conflict or the good/bad person notion. You may begin thinking that you really do not need to respect the other person's differences, and in so doing, you communicate the belief that your partner is a loser or bad (or that you yourself are that way).

Also during this phase, you can experience vulnerability to attraction to an outside alternative. It is tempting to turn to an affair or to an offer to moonlight on other jobs to escape the dissatisfying situation with your partner. Frequently the alternative is no better or worse, only different. The romance and excitement of reentering the visionary phase with a new person usually overshadows the fact that you would have to recycle the relationship phases — including the adversarial phase — with a new partner. Never really understanding this, some people run from situation to situation unable to make a commitment to work through differences effectively.

Many relationships end with the adversarial phase. Others remain stuck in this phase for long periods, bringing bitterness and underlying pain. Still other partners learn from the phase, and then move on to a new phase in their relationship.

DORMANT PHASE

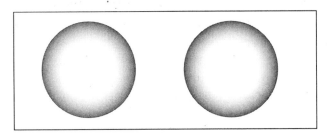

Characteristics of the Dormant Phase

Once you have survived some of the struggles characteristic of the adversarial phase, you begin to develop more acceptance of life — and more acceptance of both of you. You accept yourself for who are. You also know that your partner will not always live up to your expectations, and yet you still recognize and value your partner for who he or she is.

You enter a phase in which you have more perspective about various events connected to your relationship. Any single event, which in the past might have been potentially damaging, now probably does not threaten the relationship. You are less apt to feel hurt, anger, or discouragement by one situation. Rather, you view situations in terms of a larger whole. Surprises are few, and you know that life will go on.

You live and work more peacefully with one another, even if the peacefulness sometimes covers an inner discontent. You are aware of your patterns of behaving, and during this dormant phase, you quit pressuring one another to change. You are more congenial with each other and do not rock the boat.

Since neither of you wants to make waves, you may both avoid the conflict that may accompany dealing with real issues. Issues resolve themselves by default, or one of you capitulates quickly to the persuasion of the other. Possibly the one for whom the issue is most pressing at a particular time handles it in the most expedient way for the moment, regardless of whether it is best in the long run for your relationship.

You both maintain an obvious structural commitment to your relationship. Others take for granted your relationship to one another. You are known as a pair. But often your time together is "on automatic," such as going to social or family gatherings. The relationship continues in this condition, whether satisfactory or not, often maintained by circumstance or other values, such as religious convictions, social expectations, children, or fulfilling economic commitments.

However, you may not spend very much time together alone. Your activities and interests are more separate now. You each go your own way — in career interests, with your own friends, in community affairs, in being involved with children's activities, and so on. Any of these other parts of life can draw your energies in directions away from one another.

You probably share less of the intrinsic aspects of whatever it is that helps make life worth living for each of you. Consequently, your relationship together receives little nourishment. While other parts of life may be full and vital, during this phase the relationship stays relatively inactive and lifeless. If your relationship is basically viable, you are likely to feel peaceful and serene during this phase. Otherwise, you may feel dissatisfied and discontented about the relationship.

In this time of independence from one another, you each establish autonomy and emphasize or create your own identity. As partners, you support, or at least do not take steps to prevent, the liberty for each to rely on yourselves separately. You both direct your energy toward your individual or personal activities.

The Focus

The focus during this phase is on:
me — who I am as an individual

You and your partner develop the interests you each find important. These interests may come from other life demands (finances, education, children, community needs). You go your way, and you permit the freedom for your partner to go his or her way. You do not bother each other.

Positives and Negatives

Similar to the other phases, this dormant phase offers some positive aspects. During this time each of you can develop real individuality as an adult. You can discover strengths and explore interests, and generally do so with the security of having relationship and emotional needs already met. The phase provides a context to find out "who I am," or "what my individual style really is." That allows your partner and others to appreciate you for who you are now and not for who they thought you were or should be.

The dormant phase also provides more economy for the relationship system. Only so much energy exists in any one pair, and in busy periods many things draw on that energy. It simply makes good sense to have separate areas of concentrated attention by each partner.

Also on the positive side of this phase, you each learn to take more self-responsibility for contentment in life. Your individual personality can get full play, and you must account for it. As this occurs, you start to realize that some of your own responses to the world shape your satisfaction, and you lessen your tendency to point a finger of responsibility at your partner when something goes wrong. You accept your own strengths and limitations: You recognize where you flourish or have difficulty in meeting issues and challenges of life.

However, a negative dimension comes into the dormant phase, too. Sometimes each of you takes on so much self-responsibility for making life be the way "I want" that you shut out your partner. You can also be drawn to an outside alternative, wanting something new and special for yourself. Perhaps this is another relationship, yet you do not take steps to end the one you have with your partner, because that is comfortable and stable.

Another negative aspect of this phase occurs when personal distance from each other becomes a habit. Once your patterns of separate behavior become well established, this habit may prevent real intimacy from occurring during the dormant phase when it might otherwise be possible.

Until something brings it to life again — or until through atrophy it withers and dies — your relationship stays in the sleeplike state of dormancy. This phase can extend for years, and partners live out their lives with mild but relatively lifeless connecting. Some couples end their relationship, even after many apparently peaceful years, when they have lived and grown apart in this way.

Yet, the dormant phase can be a brief season between other phases, a necessary preparation for renewed energy and growth together. Partners take steps to make something happen for themselves as a couple.

VITAL PHASE

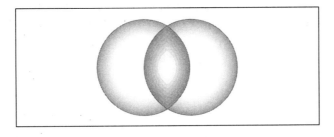

Characteristics of the Vital Phase

The vital phase usually grows out of some form of challenge to the relationship as it has been. You and your partner are faced with a question about its personal value to you. Something forces you to test its resilience. No longer can it stay quietly asleep.

A relationship may enter the vital phase at a time of high stress. For instance, it may occur when you or your partner loses a job or a major contract, when an accident or serious illness arises and forces priority-shifting, or when an opportunity comes that benefits only one of you, yet affects the other as well. Other challenges include the birth of a child, discovery of an affair, financial reversals, spiritual conversion, and retirement.

For example, "You get a job opportunity that requires you to move to another city. My best opportunities are to stay here, and neither of us wants a long distance relationship." A decision has to be made.

Sometimes, without an external challenge, you enter this phase after one or both determines (and the other agrees) that this is the way you desire to live, with the intention to enjoy your life together to the fullest extent. You come to a point of active choice, and, recognizing that each of you has options, you make a conscious decision to commit your energies to the relationship. With eyes wide open, both of you take responsibility to make it work.

Some couples choose relatively early in their relationship to live in a vital way. Increased awareness of the possibility for living more vitally, plus support and help being accessible, now more than ever before, make this phase a realistic choice sooner than once might have been expected. Resources are available for couples who desire such for their partnership.

In this phase, you place a higher value on blending as a pair and on balancing your individual similarities and differences to be mutually supportive. You recognize the complementarity of your differences and understand how both of you contribute to the vitality of your relationship.

During the vital phase, you put effort into discovering who your partner is now, and into how you are together. You see ways that your relationship system works well for you, and you take satisfaction in the life you live together. You hold a strong sense of trust of one another, whether you are together or apart.

Your commitment to your relationship is founded on knowing yourself and your partner in realistic terms. With this awareness, you truly have self-respect and respect for each other. You realize that you can be mutually honest about your own deepest truths and still appreciate one another, recognizing that together you are better than each of you is alone. In this phase, you experience a paradox of freedom: Your committed togetherness supports and nourishes each of your separate identities.

As partners, you experience your interdependence and thrive together. You each live with your own uniqueness and still involve yourself fully with that of your partner. An essential place for both of you in the partnership gives a sustaining quality to your relationship.

During the vital phase your interaction with each other increases — you pay attention and bring energy to your conversations. If you feel angry or upset, it typically signals an issue to resolve, and it poses little danger to the relationship. Conflict could be greater now than during the quiet dormant phase when you kept more personal distance. And compared to the conflicts of the adversarial phase, you usually can settle them faster, taking more responsibility for personal behavior. You collaborate more.

Considering your position in your Relationship Map, you spend most of your time, whether together or apart and initiating or responding to change, mostly in the positive climate. When it slips into the negative, you take action to prevent it from staying there and quickly return to a positive mode.

The Focus

In the vital phase, the focus is on:
who we are — what we are about in the present, together and apart

You place priority on what your relationship requires now.

Positives and Negatives

Positive outcomes of this phase include a sense of robustness and contentment with each other. You experience more wholeness from the blending of your differences and similarities, and you project less compartmentalization to others. Your vitality radiates outward to others.

As a pair, you stand together to face the pressures from the rest of the world. You use your combined force to make better, more satisfying decisions for both. Some pairs even intentionally extend their vitality into service for others.

While the positive aspects of the vital phase are predominant, the negatives that occur mainly do so outside your relationship. Others may be envious or want some of the vitality directed toward them. Perhaps you maintain a kind of selfishness (for the sake of the relationship) about time, energy, productivity, wisdom, and joy — and others may want to tap it more than it is available. You may begin to believe that you as a couple exist separately unto yourselves from the rest of the world.

CONSIDERING ALL THE PHASES

Once you gain perspective on all the phases — visionary, adversarial, dormant, and vital — it is helpful to remind yourself that can you move in and out of these phases over time. With the identification of the phase you and your partner may be experiencing now, you can reflect on its level of satisfaction for you, and then take steps to live in the phase you desire. (Recall the questionnaire that you completed at the beginning of this chapter. Score it, as shown on the following page, to help you identify your current phase.)

SCORE YOUR PHASES OF RELATIONSHIP QUESTIONNAIRE

Instructions:

1. For each item (from the Questionnaire), write in the number you circled for the item.

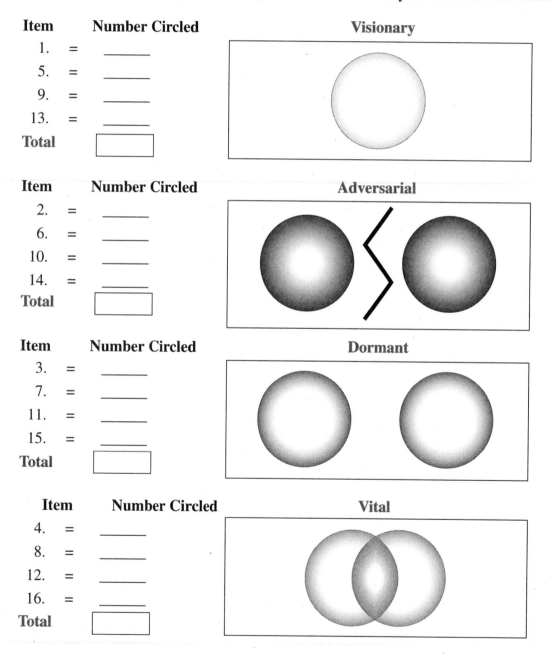

Item		**Number Circled**	**Visionary**
1.	=	_____	
5.	=	_____	
9.	=	_____	
13.	=	_____	
Total		[____]	

Item		**Number Circled**	**Adversarial**
2.	=	_____	
6.	=	_____	
10.	=	_____	
14.	=	_____	
Total		[____]	

Item		**Number Circled**	**Dormant**
3.	=	_____	
7.	=	_____	
11.	=	_____	
15.	=	_____	
Total		[____]	

Item		**Number Circled**	**Vital**
4.	=	_____	
8.	=	_____	
12.	=	_____	
16.	=	_____	
Total		[____]	

2. Add up the numbers for each set of items. The set of items with the highest number of points suggests that you are probably in that particular phase with your partner.

3. Talk with your partner about the relationship phase you are experiencing now, according to the questionnaire you completed. Are you satisfied with being in this phase? If so, you probably wish to continue in it. If not, chose the phase you want to enter.

ALIGNING YOUR RELATIONSHIP

Once you determine where you are now in relation to the phases, you have a good basis for deciding how you want to live your life together. You also possess the set of communication skills and processes that will help you through difficult aspects of a particular phase and give you the proactive ability to enter or continue in a phase in which your relationship will thrive. Choice comes with the awareness and skills.

YOUR THOUGHTS — WHAT YOU VALUE

In order for you and your partner to flourish in the context of your blended life together, it is useful to look first at your values. These are the things or qualities in life that for you hold worth for their own sake. They are intrinsically significant to you — what you think is important. Sometimes values are the parts of life that give most meaning to you.

Values fit in the thoughts zone of the Awareness Wheel. They spring from your beliefs as well as from the total of your past experiences in life.

MY VALUES

Instructions:

1. Reflect for a few moments, and then write what is important to you now, at this point in your life.

What I Value:

2. Share these values with your partner.

YOUR WANTS — WHAT YOU DESIRE

Your wants are your hopes, dreams, desires, and wishes for yourself, your partner, and your relationship together. Wants motivate you, and can propel you to move towards or away from something or someone. They can be the impetus for action.

Wants can be short-term or long-term and small or large. Whether they start as a mini-priority or a vague dream, they can blossom into a specific goal to which you aspire.

As introduced in COUPLE COMMUNICATION I, three types of wants include:
- To be — such as healthy, successful at something, a peacemaker, a leader

- To do — specifically, such as move to a different home, take a vacation, get a new job, exercise daily, or finish a project — and generally, such as volunteer, collaborate, compete, develop a deeper life of faith

- To have — such as satisfying relationships, a happy family, money in investments, a new car, a rewarding career, good friends, more time for recreational activities

When your wants are congruent with your values — with what you believe is important in life — working to gain them brings satisfaction.

However, wants can also be conflicting. Without awareness of this and by not setting priorities, they can bring internal conflict, as well as dissension between you and your partner, scattering your energy. Plus, for a relationship to thrive over time, taking account of the wants of both of you ultimately must occur.

Connecting with your wants for yourself, your partner, and your relationship allows you to set goals or objectives and helps focus your energy, so that you are more likely to achieve them. The process helps your relationship to be in alignment.

WANTS FOR MYSELF

Instructions:

1. Together with your partner, determine what you consider to be short-term and long-term time periods. Write this in the space provided below.

2. Independently, think about some of your wants for yourself, with both the short term and the long term in mind. Write this below.

	Short-Term	**Long-Term**
What time period?	_____	_____

What do I want:
   To be?

   To do (specific or general)?

   To have?

Share these wants for yourself with your partner. Then listen to your partner give his or her wants for self. Your purpose in the listening is simply to understand your partner. (Use the Listening Cycle Mat, for this part, if you wish.)

WANTS FOR MY PARTNER AND THE RELATIONSHIP

Instructions:

1. With your understanding of what your partner shared of his or her wants, consider what you want for your partner. Remember, this is not from your partner, which would be for yourself, but for your partner, based on his or her interests. This reflects your caring for your partner. (The test is: Does your partner agree that this is a want for him or her?)

2. Then also, thinking about the two of you together, reflect on what you want for your relationship. This means taking you both — your larger system — into account. What do you hope for, with you as a pair in mind?

What do I Want for:	My Partner?	For Us?
To be:		
To do:		
To have:		

3. Share with your partner your wants for him or her and your relationship.

CHOOSING FUTURE ACTIONS

Instructions: Together as partners, choose the wants to pursue now. Decide on wants for yourself, your partner, and your relationship, keeping in mind the same time periods as you determined on page 175.

Identify the next steps to make these wants a reality.

	What will I do?	**By when?**

1. For myself:

2. For my partner:

3. For us?

THRIVING TOGETHER

For a relationship to flourish and thrive over a lifetime, in the context of the complicated world in which we live, it takes a combination of qualities and abilities within the partners.

Couples who do thrive possess many of the characteristics below. Consider if you also possess:

- A caring attitude toward self and your partner

- Awareness of your own experience

- Talking skills to share your experience when it is important

- Listening skills to tune into your partner

- A conflict-resolving process

- Understanding of communication styles and how they impact your connecting or disengaging with one another

- Recognition of the climate of your relationship when you are together, apart, or initiating and responding to change

- The ability to negotiate differences with collaborative communication

- A process to manage your own anger

- A process to respond to your partner's anger to de-escalate it

- Understanding of how relationships typically change over time

- Determination to be proactive about setting goals and choosing how you want to live and relate

The objective of COUPLE COMMUNICATION has been to help you gain or improve these abilities. As a couple, you can continue to develop them, reflect on their impact, and encourage one another in their application, throughout your lives together.

Chapter References

CHAPTER 1

1. B. Hafen, K. Karren, K. Frandsen, and N. Smith, *Mind/Body Health: The Effects of Attitudes, Emotions, and Relationships*, (Boston: Allyn and Bacon, 1996); D. Ornish, *Love and Survival: The Scientific Basis for the Healing Power of Intimacy*, (New York: HarperCollins Publishers, 1997).

2. B. Hafen, K. Karren, K. Frandsen, and N. Smith, *Mind/Body Health: The Effects of Attitudes, Emotions, and Relationships*, (Boston: Allyn and Bacon, 1996).

3. B. Hafen, K. Karren, K. Frandsen, and N. Smith, *Mind/Body Health: The Effects of Attitudes, Emotions, and Relationships*, (Boston: Allyn and Bacon, 1996).

4. J. Jemmott, "Social Motives and Susceptibility to Disease: Stalking Individual Differences in Health Risks," *Journal of Personality*, 55 (1987), 267-298; L. Peplau and D. Perlman, *Loneliness: A Sourcebook of Current Theory, Research and Therapy*, (New York: Wiley-Interscience, 1982); D. Ornish, *Love and Survival: The Scientific Basis for the Healing Power of Intimacy,* (New York: HarperCollins Publishers, 1997).

5. A. Christensen, and J. Shenk, "Communication, Conflict, and Psychological Distance in Nondistressed, Clinic, and Divorcing Couples," *Journal of Consulting and Clinical Psychology*, 59 (1991), 458-463; J. Gottman, "Predicting Marital Happiness and Stability from Newlywed Interaction, *Journal of Marriage and the Family,* 60 (1998) No. 1, 5-22; J. Gottman, *Why Marriages Succeed or Fail,* (New York: Simon & Schuster, 1994).

6. P. Shaver, and C. Hazan, "Adult Romantic Attachment: Theory and Evidence," *Advances in Personal Relationships*, 4 (1993), 29-70.

7. D. Olson, J. DeFrain, *Marriage and the Family: Diversity and Strength,* (Mountain View, CA: Mayfield Publishing, 2000).

CHAPTER 2

1. S. Miller, P. Miller, E. Nunnally, D Wackman, *Talking and Listening Together: COUPLE COMMUNICATION I*, (Evergreen, Colorado: Interpersonal Communication Programs, Inc., 1991).

CHAPTER 3

1. L. Bilodeau, *The Anger Workbook*, (Minneapolis: CompCare Publishers, 1992; C. Tavris, *Anger: The Misunderstood Emotion*, (New York: Simon & Schuster, 1989); B. Bushman, R. Baumeister, and A. Stack, "Catharsis, Aggression, and Persuasive Influence: Self-Fulfilling or Self-Defeating Prophecies?" *Journal of Personality and Social Psychology*, 76 (1999), 367-376.

2. B. Hafen, K. Karren, K. Frandsen, and N. Smith, *Mind/Body Health: The Effects of Attitudes, Emotions, and Relationships*, (Boston: Allyn and Bacon, 1996); D. Ornish, *Love and Survival: The Scientific Basis for the Healing Power of Intimacy*, (New York: HarperCollins Publishers, 1997).

3. B. Hafen, K.Karren, K Frandsen, and N. Smith, *Mind/Body Health: The Effects of Attitudes, Emotions, and Relationships*, (Boston: Allyn and Bacon, 1996).

4. B. Bushman, R. Baumeister, and A. Stack, "Catharsis, Aggression, and Persuasive Influence: Self-Fulfilling or Self-Defeating Prophecies?" *Journal of Personality and Social Psychology*, 76 (1999), 367-376.

5. C. Tavris, *Anger: The Misunderstood Emotion*, (New York: Simon & Schuster, 1989).

6. B. Bushman, R. Baumeister, and A. Stack, "Catharsis, Aggression, and Persuasive Influence: Self-Fulfilling or Self-Defeating Prophecies?" *Journal of Personality and Social Psychology*, 76 (1999), 367-376.

CHAPTER 4

1. S. Miller, P. Miller, E. Nunnally, D Wackman, *Talking and Listening Together: COUPLE COMMUNICATION I*, (Evergreen, Colorado: Interpersonal Communication Programs, Inc., 1991).

CHAPTER 5

1. S. Miller, D. Wackman, E. Nunnally, and P. Miller, *Connecting With Self and Others*, (Evergreen, Colorado: Interpersonal Communication Programs, Inc., 1992).

Other Resources for Couples

PREPARE: for Engaged Couples
ENRICH: for Married Couples

PREPARE and ENRICH are two tools we recommend for systematically assessing your issues as a couple. The instruments provide feedback on strengths and work areas in your relationship. To take either instrument, you and your partner each complete a questionnaire that is then computer scored. You receive feedback in the following areas: leisure activities, realistic expectations (in Prepare only), marital satisfaction (in Enrich only), personality issues, communication, conflict, family and friends, children and parenting, egalitarian roles, religious orientation, financial management, sexual relationship, cohesion and adaptability.

For more information on PREPARE or ENRICH, contact:

> **Life Innovations, Inc.**
> P. O. Box 190
> Minneapolis, MN 55440-0190
> 1-800-331-1661

THE ASSOCIATION FOR COUPLES IN MARRIAGE ENRICHMENT

ACME is an international organization committed to helping couples develop the skills needed to improve their relationships. The Association provides retreats, workshops, learning events, and resources for couples.

For the name and address of an ACME contact person in your area, write or call:

> **ACME**
> 459 South Church Street
> P.O. Box 10596
> Winston-Salem, North Carolina 27108
> 1-800-634-8325

Also Available from ICP, Inc.

If you have found the Couple Communication Program useful, consider these other related programs and materials from Interpersonal Communication Programs, Inc. (ICP):

CORE COMMUNICATION: SKILLS AND PROCESSES

CORE COMMUNICATION is for individuals who want to talk and listen more effectively, resolve conflicts/issues better, and facilitate collaborative interactions between others. In addition to skill development, CORE COMMUNICATION teaches specific communication principles, such as reading nonverbal messages, building rapport, and reducing resistance. It also covers processes for responding to Fight Talk, Spite Talk, and Mixed Messages.

COLLABORATIVE TEAM SKILLS

This program teaches groups who work together the same maps, skills, and processes that COUPLE COMMUNICATION I offers to partners. Participants use their own and their groups' real issues as they learn how to communicate about situations and resolve conflicts more effectively. COLLABORATIVE TEAM SKILLS is useful in the following contexts:

- Team Building
- Staff Development
- Implementation of Self-Directed Work Teams

For More Information on the cost, availability of materials, and training, contact:

> **Interpersonal Communication Programs, Inc.**
> 30752 Southview Drive, Suite 200
> Evergreen, Colorado 80439
> Toll-free: 800-328-5099
> Fax: 303-674-4283
> Email: icp@comskills.com
> Web: www.couplecommunication.com